Seinfeld and Philosophy

2000

Dear Allan,

I thought for sure you
would have written this one!

Merry Christmas
and love,

Joanne
and
Tommy

Seinfeld and Philosophy

A Book about Everything and Nothing

Edited by
WILLIAM IRWIN

OPEN COURT
Chicago and La Salle, Illinois

To order books from Open Court, call 1-800-815-2280.

Seinfeld cast cover photograph: Gino Misfed/Shooting Star. © All rights reserved.

Open Court Publishing Company is a division of Carus Publishing Company.

© 2000 by Carus Publishing Company

First printing 2000
Second printing 2000

Printed and bound in the United States of America.

Library of Congress Cataloging-in-Publication Data

Seinfeld and philosophy : a book about everything and nothing / edited by William Irwin.
    p.   cm.
    Includes bibliographical references and index.
    ISBN 0-8126-9409-0 (alk. paper)
    1. Philosophy—Miscellanea. 2. Seinfeld. (Television program)—Miscellanea.   I. Irwin, William, 1970–
    B68 .S44 1999
    100—dc21   99-15910
                                                                   CIP

Dedicated to Bob Sacamano

Contents

Act III
Untimely Meditations by the Water Cooler   119

Act IV
Is there Anything Wrong with That?   161

Preface

The writing, editing, and other miscellaneous tasks involved in assembling *Seinfeld and Philosophy: A Book about Everything and Nothing* were a terrific and unparalleled experience. Each of the contributors was a consummate professional, working hard, paying diligent attention to details, and keeping a sense of humor throughout. The good folks at Open Court, David Ramsay Steele in particular, were a pleasure to work with, and are to be thanked and congratulated for having the fortitude, vision, and sense of humor to publish this volume.

In addition to the contributors and the publisher I wish to thank all those with whom I have discussed the connections between philosophy and *Seinfeld*. Many of these individuals took the time to read drafts of early versions of the essays in this book, offering valuable comments and criticisms which no doubt improved the final product. A list such as this is inevitably incomplete, but among those to whom I am indebted are: Gregory Bassham, Derrick Boucher, Alan Clune, Jason Goodman, Robert Guldner, Kathleen Irwin, Mary Ellen Irwin, William N. Irwin, Megan Lloyd, JR Lombardo, Jennifer O'Neill, Marc Marchese, Troy Marziotti, Henry Nardone, Joseph Schmidt, Kate Williams, all members of the original Buffalo Rectangle, and my colleagues and students at King's College.

Monologue
Seinfeld, "The Field of Being"

WILLIAM IRWIN

Why a book on philosophy and *Seinfeld?* How can philosophy, the discipline which is "a more or less general theory of everything" deal with a show which claims to be "about nothing"? Well, allow me to suggest that everything and nothing are sometimes not so terribly far apart. To put it more correctly, the "nothing" that *Seinfeld* deals with is most definitely something, something at times philosophical. The most popular sitcom of the 1990s managed to draw life's everyday events to our attention in a way not often done before, highlighting the commonplace and mundane, drawing our attention to things that would otherwise go unnoticed. Socrates told us that "the unexamined life is not worth living." The characters on *Seinfeld* certainly examine their own lives, though I doubt Socrates would find much to approve of in their lives or their examinations!

This "show about nothing" is indeed philosophical in its own way. The very name 'Seinfeld' rings with philosophical significance, calling to mind (for some of us, at least) Martin Heidegger's *Sein und Zeit (Being and Time),* and meaning (roughly) "field of being" in German. *Seinfeld* has indeed been fertile ground, a "field of being" from which spring fruitful discussions and observations of the philosophical importance of the mundane. As a teacher, I have found *Seinfeld* to be an invaluable pedagogical tool. Tough philosophical issues easily come to life on the *Seinfeld* stage. For example, many times I have said to my students that when Heidegger speaks of the "idle chatter" of the "inauthentic mode of being" just think of Jerry, George, Elaine, and Kramer sitting at their favorite booth in Monk's Coffee Shop discussing some trivial piece of nonsense. To take another example, I tell my students that philosophy asks us to look at life in ways different from those to which we are accustomed. Changing one's ways of viewing the world and acting upon those changes takes a certain amount of courage, but the payoff can be fantastic. Just think of what happens when George asks himself, "What is the opposite of what I would normally do?", and then acts on his answer. In turn my students have often drawn examples of the show's relevance to my attention. Indeed, class discussions and student term paper examples in my Existentialism course inspired me to write my essay for this volume, "Kramer and Kierkegaard: Stages on Life's Way." For those discussions and examples I am truly grateful. The philosophical relevance of *Seinfeld* goes beyond the classroom, however. Examples, such as those that the show provides, are often a key to understanding for both the novice and the expert in philosophy.

We should note that Friedrich Nietzsche gave his *Thus Spoke Zarathustra* the subtitle "A Book for None and All." The subtitle of *Seinfeld and Philosophy* is "A Book about Everything and Nothing." This, of course, alludes to the paradoxical subtitle of Nietzsche's masterpiece, but it also raises the question: Who is this book for? *Seinfeld and Philosophy* is for the "educated" *Seinfeld* fan, schooled in philosophy or steeped in *Seinfeld*. Some readers will be educated in both philosophy and *Seinfeld* and perhaps some will be educated in neither, *not that there's anything wrong with that*. Anyone who has ever spent too much time by the water cooler discussing either 'Must See TV' or the mysteries of the universe will find much of interest herein. The essays are written with the intent that they be accessible to the student or non-philosopher, but yet of interest to those educated in philosophy as well. The essays are not written with the hope of capturing the meaning that the authors of the episodes may have had in mind. Rather, they are written to highlight the philosophical significance of the show.

The idea for this book occurred to me after attending the annual Eastern Division Meeting of the American Philosophical Association, perhaps the most important philosophical gathering of the year in this country. A number of colleagues and I had our usual discussions about the state of the profession, the job market, our respective institutions, *yada yada yada*. Also, of course, we discussed *Seinfeld,* and, in truth, we discussed *Seinfeld* more than anything else. The news had just broken that the show was going off the air, and, to say the least, we were disappointed. Why? Not just because the show had become a fixture in our lives, but because we sensed that something quite relevant and, yes, philosophical was about to be lost.

The contributors to this volume are *Seinfeld* fans who teach and write in the area of philosophy; together they represent a diversity of philosophical perspectives, traditions, and orientations. The reader should note that the essays are grouped in four *acts*. Act I, "The Characters," comprises four essays, each of which looks at a different member of the "Fab Four" through philosophical lenses. Act II, "*Seinfeld* and the Philosophers," consists of four essays, each of which looks at a historical philosopher, or philosophy, through *Seinfeld*ian lenses. Act III, "Untimely Meditations by the Water Cooler," comprises three essays, each of which explores a philosophical issue raised by the show, for example, is it rational for George to "do the opposite"? And Act IV, "Is there Anything Wrong with That?" consists of three essays, each of which explores ethical issues, using *Seinfeld* as its basis.

The Characters, aka "The New York Four"

1
Jerry and Socrates: The Examined Life?

WILLIAM IRWIN

It is only appropriate to begin this book on philosophy and *Seinfeld* with a look at the character Jerry (1989–1998 A.C.E.) and the philosopher Socrates (470–399 B.C.E.). There would be no show without both the character Jerry Seinfeld and the man by the same name. It is also true that there would be no philosophy as we know it today without the philosopher Socrates and his student and biographer, Plato (428–348 B.C.E.).

Introductory philosophy courses frequently begin by examining the Socratic dialogues of Plato, the dramatic play-like works in which Socrates is featured as the main character. At first glance Jerry and Socrates might seem to be as far apart as can possibly be, but with a little exploration we can see that this in fact is not the case. In this essay, then, we shall compare and contrast Jerry and Socrates, and, in doing so, shed some light on both of them.

The Jerry Problem and The Socratic Problem

Our first point of comparison between Jerry and Socrates is the relationship between reality and fiction in *Seinfeld* and in the writings of Plato. When NBC first approached Jerry Seinfeld about doing a television show he was eager to accept but without any definite ideas for what it should be about. He called up his friend and colleague Larry David, a comedian with a dark sense of humor and known in the business as a comedian's comedian. Seinfeld and David sat down, perhaps at a booth in a coffee shop, not unlike the fictional Monk's. David suggested that the show should be based on Jerry himself, a comedian living in New York. This idea had its advantages. It did not call for much imagination, or perhaps so it seemed, and it did not require that Jerry play a person he was not. Jerry had done a short stint on the sitcom *Benson,* but was not entirely comfortable with acting. The idea of playing himself was attractive to Seinfeld, but would it work? Would anyone find it funny? Who else would be in the show? The other three primary characters also have their roots in reality. George is sometimes said to be the dark side or *id* of Larry David, with his worries, neuroses, and schemes. Cosmo Kramer was based on Kenny Kramer, a long-time eccentric neighbor of Larry David. And Elaine, who was added to the show only after the first episode, is to some extent based on comedienne Carol Leifer, the friend and ex-girlfriend of the real Jerry.

The many connections between the fictional show and the reality on which it is based are well known to fans. Kenny Kramer, for example, has started the "Kramer Reality Tour" in Manhattan to highlight his own significance. In a bit of fiction vs. reality ping-pong, the show countered with an episode in which Cosmo Kramer started his own "Peterman Reality Tour" after selling his life stories to J. Peterman. The question we shall examine briefly, however, is this: Is the fictional Jerry Seinfeld the actual Jerry Seinfeld? The easy answer would be no. One is a character on TV and one is a real person. This much is true, and certainly parts of Jerry the character's personality are exaggerated for comic effect, his obsessive neatness and his fickleness with women for example. Still, the two are remarkably similar. A strange twist on this question was generated by the publication of the bestseller *Seinlanguage.* This book was written and published by the actual Jerry Seinfeld, but nearly all its contents first became known to the public as the words of the character Jerry Seinfeld. That is to say, *Seinlanguage* consists largely of transcribed stand-up comedy routines that readers will recognize as having been delivered by the fictional Jerry Seinfeld on stage during his comedy routines on the show. So, whose words are these? The real Jerry's or the fictional Jerry's? Clearly the real Jerry was (largely) responsible for writing them even if they were first known to the public as lines in the comedy routine of a fictional character. Still, the actual person Jerry Seinfeld subsequently makes these lines available in print, this time presumably to be taken as his own words in his own voice.

I do not hope or plan to settle this issue but simply want to point to its strange and convoluted nature. For the most part, we can assume that the fictional Jerry is not exactly the same as the real Jerry, though he is based on him to a large extent. Sometimes the two will be far apart, but sometimes they will indeed be almost one and the same.

This discussion of fiction and reality with Jerry leads us to the relationship between fiction and reality in the works of Plato. Socrates was, in an unconventional sense, the teacher of Plato. Socrates, however, wrote nothing, and so we know of his life and philosophy almost exclusively through the writings of Plato. Plato was inspired by the words and deeds of the master, so much so that he gave up his other interests in politics and poetry to become a philosopher. After the death of Socrates, Plato ensured that the former's legacy would live on by incorporating Socrates as a character in his writings. As we shall discuss shortly, Plato wrote dialogues, what may be thought of, in a loose sense, as philosophical plays in which characters exchange speeches. Socrates is nearly always the main character and winner of the debate in the Platonic dialogues. This situation, much as the Jerry vs. Jerry situation, poses a problem. How do we know what Socrates said and thought as opposed to what Plato said and thought? Or, where do the ideas of Socrates leave off and those of Plato begin? This is a complicated scholarly issue, one which is not firmly settled.[1] It has been called "The Socratic Problem." Luckily, there is no need for us to solve the Socratic problem here. We simply need to be aware that when we discuss the words of Socrates these words may actually be expressing the thoughts of Plato.

---

[1] Scholars usually divide the Platonic dialogues into three groups. The first group, the early dialogues, is believed to be based largely on the words and deeds of Socrates. The second group, the middle dialogues, contains a mixture of the thoughts of both Socrates and Plato. The third group, the late dialogues, contains the mature thought of Plato. Things are not as straightforward as this simple categorization might imply, however.

The Life and Death of Socrates

Socrates was, in many ways, a rare individual. He may be classed among such other seminal thinkers as Jesus, Buddha, and Gandhi whose lives were practically inseparable from their philosophies. We cannot say for certain that all of Socrates' important life events and philosophy have been passed on through the writings of Plato, but we can be fairly confident that Plato's *Apology* is an accurate account of Socrates's words and actions at the trial where he was falsely accused, charged with impiety and corrupting the youth, and ultimately, sentenced to death. Let us get a feel for the spirit of Socrates by examining some of his words during that trial. Note his unwillingness to compromise himself, his commitment to his principles, and his serenity in the face of death.

> I am not upset, men of Athens, at what has just happened—your finding me guilty . . . (*Apology* 35e)[2]

> I tried to persuade each of you not to give any thought to his own affairs until he had first given some thought to himself, and tried to make himself as good and wise as possible; not to give any thought to the affairs of the city without first giving some thought to the city itself; and to observe the same priorities in other areas as well. What then do I deserve for behaving like this? Something good, men of Athens, if I am really supposed to make a proposal in accordance with what I deserve. (*Apology* 36d) So if I must propose a penalty based on justice, on what I deserve, then that's what I propose—free meals at the public expense. (*Apology* 36e)

> I have lost my case, not for want of a speech, but for want of effrontery and shamelessness, for refusing to make the kind of a speech you most enjoy listening to. (*Apology* 35e)

> You too, men of the jury, must not be apprehensive about death. You must regard one thing at least as certain—that no harm can come to a good man either in his life or after his death. (*Apology* 41d)

---

[2] Italicized words refer to the titles of Plato's dialogues. Numbers and letters refer to scholarly section markers which are reprinted in all available editions and translations of Plato's dialogues.

I must stop. It is time for us to go—me to my death, you to your lives. Which of us goes to the better fate, only god knows. (*Apology* 42a)

As you can gather, Socrates was a man dedicated to his principles and to improving the lives of others by making them look at themselves. At this point, it may not sound as if he has a lot in common with Jerry Seinfeld, but, as we shall see, there are some similarities in their approaches to life.

Jerry and Socrates, Flies on a Horse's Ass

Socrates tells us that "the greatest good in a man's life is this, to be each day discussing human excellence and other subjects you hear me talking about, examining myself and other people . . . *the unexamined life isn't worth living*" (*Apology* 38a). Indeed, Socrates lived by these words, spending his days in the marketplace trying to bring important subjects to the attention of the citizens of Athens. Often, however, these people did not appreciate the efforts of Socrates, a fact that did not escape his attention. Still, he felt it was his duty to awaken his fellow citizens, who were, as he saw it, sleepwalking through life. They were caught up in the everyday affairs of business and politics and had lost sight of themselves and their place in the community. They failed to address that most basic philosophical question: *What is the good life?* The city of Athens was at a political and cultural high point, yet the handwriting on the wall, at least as Socrates read it, foretold disaster. The citizens each had to make themselves better if there was to be a hope for the future of Athens. Socrates saw it as his divine command to rouse the city into action, as a gadfly (or horsefly) rouses a sleepy horse on a hot summer day.

It is as if the city, to use a slightly absurd simile, were a horse—a large horse, high mettled, but which because of its size is somewhat sluggish, and needs to be stung into action by some kind of horsefly. I think god has caused me to settle on the city as this horsefly, the sort that never stops, all day long, coming to rest on every part of you, stinging each one of you into action, and persuading and criticizing each one of you. (*Apology* 30e)

With this kind of action, it is no wonder that Socrates made a few enemies. (Jesus, of course, was not universally well liked either.) He was forcing the people to examine their own lives, a task none too easy with oftentimes-unhappy results.

Jerry may not be the same kind of impetus to thought that Socrates was, but I would suggest that there is some similarity between the roles Socrates and Jerry played in their communities. Jerry, like Socrates, provokes his friends and his audience by bringing to mind subjects to which they would not ordinarily give much thought. Like Socrates, Jerry also assembles a band of followers who mimic his style of questioning and concern. George, Elaine, and Kramer feed into his observational questioning and humor. George and Elaine, it seems, would be lost without it, and in fact cannot even successfully interact with one another outside the presence of Jerry. Of course, we must be careful not to overstate the similarity here. Socrates is concerned with questions of the good life and human excellence, whereas Jerry is occupied with questions like: Is soup a meal? What are the rules for breaking up with someone over the phone?, and, does Superman have a super sense of humor?

Another important difference between Jerry and Socrates is their appraisal of their own knowledge. For Socrates, questions are at least as important as answers. If one does not ask, for example, What is the good life?, what chance is there that one will ever find it? Socrates, in addition to characterizing himself as a gadfly, portrays himself as a midwife, one who does not give birth but aids in the birthing process. He claims to know nothing, but at least he is aware of that fact. He portrays his role as one who can get others to see what they know, by asking them questions and eliciting responses. In contrast, Jerry seems to have a much higher opinion of his own level of knowledge. Often as part of his stand-up routine, Jerry asks and answers his own questions. "I did this whole thing on the Ottoman Empire. Like, what was this? A whole empire based on putting your feet up" ("The Non-Fat Yogurt")?[3] Or, "Why would I be a leg man? I don't need legs. I have legs" ("The Implant"). He can also be quite smug, and clearly thinks he is better off than his friends.

---

[3] See the Episode Guide at the end of this volume for an ordered list of the episodes.

In his most famous work, the *Republic*, Plato has Socrates tell a story which has become known as the allegory of the cave (514a–521b). For the sake of telling the story and discussing the philosophical theory it embodies, we will speak as if the words and ideas are those of Socrates, though, as we know, Plato may simply be using him as a mouthpiece for his own ideas. As the story goes, there are a group of prisoners chained by the neck, hands, and legs who watch shadows on the wall of the cave in which they are imprisoned. They have been this way since birth and so have no conception of any other way of life. The shadows are created through the aid of light from a fire and figures of animals which are passed before the fire in the manner of a puppet show. These prisoners, then, are watching shadows on a wall, yet they are not even the shadows of real things but of carved figures, and the light which makes these shadows possible is fire light, not the best possible kind of light, sunlight. These prisoners do not know that they are prisoners and do not suspect that there is any reality but the reality they know, the shadows on the wall. They do not know of anything else and accept this life as the only one possible. One day, however, one of the prisoners is set free of his chains, is taken to the outside world, and by the light of the sun beholds things as they actually are. Rather than selfishly remaining in the outside world, the prisoner returns to tell others and lead them to this greater plane of being. The others are, of course, resistant, believing that the returning prisoner has gone mad. (He cannot see properly in the cave after all, accustomed as he has become to the light of the sun.) Despite the difficulty he knows he will face and does indeed face, the prisoner feels obligated to make the return and share what he has learned. This story, in some way, parallels the life of Socrates who was thought mad and ultimately put to death for trying to draw attention to such a higher plane of thought and reality.

Plato also has the Socrates character give voice to one of the most important and influential theories in the history of thought, the theory of the Forms. Socrates (or, at least, Plato speaking through Socrates) claims that there are different levels of reality in our universe, just as there are different levels of reality in the universe of the prisoners in the cave. We are not so unlike the prisoners, as it turns out, for we often arrogantly take for granted and suppose that the reality in which we live is the truest and highest reality there is. Not so, claims Socrates. There is a higher level of reality, the level of ultimate reality as possessed by the ideal Forms. Socrates claims that all we know in this world, on this level of reality, are poor imitations of the Forms. We may experience things such as beauty, justice, and goodness, but all of these things are mere imitations of the perfect Forms, copies of Beauty itself, Justice itself, *yada yada yada*. Let's take a look at an excerpt from the *Republic* in which Socrates discusses the forms with one of his dialogue partners.

> SOCRATES: Do we say there is such a thing as the Just itself, or not?
>
> SIMMIAS: We do say so, by Zeus.
>
> SOCRATES: And the Beautiful, and the Good?
>
> SIMMIAS: Of course.
>
> SOCRATES: And have you ever seen any of these things with your eyes?
>
> SIMMIAS: In no way . . .
>
> SOCRATES: Or have you ever grasped them with any of your bodily senses? I am speaking of all such things as Size, Health, Strength, and, in a word, the reality of all other things, that which each of them essentially is. Is what is most true in them contemplated through the body, or is this the position: whoever of us prepares himself best and most accurately to grasp the thing itself which he is investigating will come closest to the knowledge of it?
>
> SIMMIAS: Obviously.
>
> SOCRATES: Then he will do this most perfectly who approaches the object with thought alone, without associating any sight with his thought, or dragging in any sense perception with his reasoning, but who, using thought alone, tries to track down each reality pure and by itself, freeing himself as far as possible from eyes and ears, and in a word, from the whole body, because the body confuses the soul . . . (*Republic* 475 e–476 a)

As this discussion suggests, Socrates holds that the body gets in the way of "knowing" the Forms. It is the soul, rather than the body, which is best suited for apprehending the Forms. There is, then, a perfect Form of Beauty, and a perfect Form of Justice, and a perfect Form of Goodness, and so on. We should, then, according to Socrates, concern ourselves with the nature of the Forms. And this leads him to ask his dialogue partners many questions in the form of, what is X? What is Justice? What is Beauty? What is Goodness? What is Virtue? What is Piety? *Yada yada yada.* Consider, as an example of this type of questioning, this discussion from Plato's dialogue *The Euthyphro.* Here Socrates and Euthyphro begin to discuss the question, What is Piety?

> SOCRATES: Now, therefore, please explain to me what you were so confident just now that you knew. Tell me what are righteousness and sacrilege with respect to murder and everything else. I suppose that piety is the same in all actions and that impiety is always the opposite of piety, and retains its identity, and that, as impiety, it always has the same character, which will be found in whatever is impious.
>
> EUTHYPHRO: Certainly, Socrates, I suppose so.
>
> SOCRATES: Tell me, then, what is piety and what is impiety? (*Euthyphro* 5d)

We should note the parallel in the way Jerry's humorous inquiries often take the form of questions. He too is looking for the nature or essence of things. Consider these bits of wisdom from Jerry on the nature of giving, Christmas, the black and white cookie, and the right to pee.

> JERRY: Are you even vaguely familiar with the concept of giving? There's no grace period.
>
> GEORGE: Well, didn't he re-gift the label maker?
>
> JERRY: Possibly.
>
> GEORGE: Well, if he can re-gift, why can't you de-gift? ("The Label Maker")

> That's the true spirit of Christmas, people being helped by people other than me. ("The Pick")

The key to eating a black and white cookie, Elaine, is you want to get some black and some white in each bite. Nothing mixes better than vanilla and chocolate. And yet, still, somehow racial harmony eludes us. If people would only look to the cookie all our problems would be solved. ("The Dinner Party")

There's too much urinary freedom in this society. I'm proud to hold it in. It builds character. ("The Parking Garage")

Both Socrates and Seinfeld manage to make something considerable out of seemingly obvious questions and trivial subject matter.

Socrates and Seinfeld are also both fond of using irony. What is irony? In the movie *Reality Bites* a very bright young college grad, played by Wynona Rider, blows the final question on a job interview when she is unable to give a definition of irony. She seeks comfort in her slacker friend, played by Ethan Hawke, asking him if he can believe it—they actually asked her to define irony! He responds, "That's when the actual meaning is the exact opposite of the literal meaning." And he is correct, if not complete, in his definition.

Socrates may, to some extent, be said to be ironic when he claims to know nothing, despite seeming to possess great knowledge. For another example, consider how he taunts his accusers by asking for free meals at the public expense as his penalty for the charges of which he is found guilty. (Though, to some extent, he is quite literally minded here as well.) In the *Republic* Socrates poses the question: What is Justice? His style, of course, is to ask others questions, claiming not to know the answers himself. His irony is not lost on some of his dialogue partners, however. Consider this excerpt from the *Republic* in which Thrasymachus gets fed up with Socrates' irony: "[T]here you go again with your old affectation, Socrates. I knew it, and I told the others that you would never let yourself be questioned, but go on shamming ignorance and do anything rather than give a straight answer" (*Republic* 337a). Jerry, like Socrates, often speaks ironically and in fact at times sarcastically. He knows it too. "I can't go to a bad movie by myself. What, am I gonna make sarcastic remarks to strangers" ("The Chinese Restaurant")? Some of Jerry's most frequent refrains are ironic, if not sarcastic. When Kramer proposes a new hare-brained scheme, Jerry is often content to simply respond "Oh, that'll work," or "that's nice." Think for example of the time when he tells Elaine with a straight face that Tolstoy had originally wanted to entitle his magnum opus not *War and Peace,* but *War: What Is It Good For?* ("The Marine Biologist") There is a real danger in not detecting irony, as one usually ends up looking like a fool. Socrates' undetected irony so often makes his dialogue partners look foolish that we can have no doubt that he made plenty of enemies this way. When Elaine takes Jerry literally on this occasion she ends up telling both her boss at Pendant Publishing and an important Russian novelist that Tolstoy did indeed want to entitle his masterpiece just that, *War: What Is It Good For?* The lesson to be learned: keep your irony radar on at all times when reading Plato and watching *Seinfeld.* We should also note that both Socrates and Seinfeld illustrate that the distinctions among irony, sarcasm, lying, and being a smart-ass are not always crystal clear!

The Fates of Socrates and Seinfeld

As we have noted, Socrates meets his death as a result of a dubious conviction, and yet he remains true to his principles and beliefs to the very end. In the *Phaedo* Plato relates the story of Socrates's final day on earth, a short time after his trial, a day during which he faces death itself with the same serenity that he faced his conviction and sentencing. In fact, he spends his final hours comforting his followers, assuring them that the soul is immortal and that he will live on, that he is going to a far better place. Certainly, I have not and cannot do justice to the majestically admirable way Socrates lived his life and accepted his death, but anyone who has ever had the life-altering experience of reading the Platonic dialogues can have no doubt that the words of his follower were true: "That . . . was the death of our friend. Of the men of his time that we knew, he was the best, we would claim, and in general, the wisest and most just" (*Phaedo* 118a). Indeed, Socrates should be counted among Jesus, Buddha, and Gandhi as archetypes of the examined and well-lived life. His impression and his influence are, with good reason, enduring.

The character Jerry Seinfeld, on the other hand, lives an examined life, but by no means an exemplary life. At the beginning of the series, Jerry appeared to be pretty much the "normal one" of the group. At least, George and Kramer in particular seemed wacky by comparison. As the series progressed, however, so did Jerry's faults. He is neurotic, fickle, and obsessively neat. He may have some primitive moral code, or at least a sense of etiquette, but he is totally self-absorbed. He is not, as Socrates was, more concerned with others than with himself. Far from it. In the final episode, Jerry along with the others, is convicted for violating a Good Samaritan Law, failing to come to the rescue of a car-jacking victim.[4] He is selfish to the end, enjoying the mugging as a spectacle. Like Socrates, he remains himself to the end but, in this case, this is not entirely a good thing. The series closes with Jerry attempting to bring his stand up "gadfly" routine to the prison inmates. Jerry in the end, though perhaps not despicable, is not to be emulated or admired.

Having looked at the central character in *Seinfeld* and *the* seminal philosopher in the Western tradition, we are now prepared to take a look at the other characters, consider other philosophers, and begin to look at the worlds of pop culture and academic philosophy through a new set of glasses.[5]

---

[4] For some discussion as to whether Jerry and the others were fairly convicted see Theodore Schick, Jr.'s "The Final Episode: Is Doing Nothing Something?" the final essay in this volume.

[5] I wish to thank Sarah Worth and Greg Bassham for valuable comments on an earlier version of this essay.

2
George's Failed Quest for Happiness: An Aristotelian Analysis

DANIEL BARWICK

Of the four main characters on *Seinfeld*, George is clearly the loser. His misfortunes are not the result of bad luck, however. Nor are they the result of his many failed relationships or his sad physical condition. Rather, they are a direct and ongoing consequence of his pathetic personality. His baseline state of perpetual melancholy and cynicism is punctuated by bouts of rage (usually against those whom he perceives are persecuting him in some way and usually misplaced), obsession (perhaps with his weight, baldness, a woman, or a new pastime such as parking cars for a living), lust (usually satisfied vicariously through Jerry or Kramer), and deep depression (usually necessitating a trip to the beach, where George goes to think his most despondent thoughts). His miserable existence is alleviated only rarely by even the most transient happiness; even in such cases, we see that George's joy (usually centering on some victory over a perceived enemy) is forced and hollow. I shall presuppose in this paper that the reader is familiar with these aspects of George's personality. If by chance you are a *Seinfeld* neophyte, take my word for it: George is a failure, a flop, a nonstarter, a paradigm of inefficacy, sloth, and incontinence.

Aristotle taught that the soul of every person has a rational aspect (the province of what he calls intellectual virtue). This rational aspect of the soul has two parts; one devoted to theoretical wisdom, and the other devoted to practical wisdom.

George seems to have neither. Although we may think that deep within every man is the capacity for virtuous, rational thought, George seems unique, in that his actions spring not from virtue or reason, but instead from the wildly fluctuating inclinations of a lunatic, driven mad by decades of hair loss, obesity, sexual dysfunction (or at least scarcity), and the relentless din of his screaming parents.

George is one of what Aristotle calls "the many," a phrase representing the view of the ordinary person. (Aristotle contrasts "the many" with "the wise", so it seems safe to say that Aristotle would not think George is wise, although he probably wouldn't be disagreeing with anyone on that.) Aristotle would have been happy to know of George, for George is a sort of paradigm case of "the many", with all of the deficiencies of many people rolled into one, and thus provides an excellent example of how not to live one's life.

Occasionally (typically following a beach visit or rejection by the fair sex), George considers his lot in life. We see a good example of this in "The Opposite":

GEORGE: (sighs) It isn't working.

JERRY: What is it that isn't working?

GEORGE: Why did it all turn out like this for me? I had so much promise. I was personable, I was bright . . . oh, not academically speaking, but I was perceptive. I always know when someone's uncomfortable at a party. It all became very clear as I was sitting out there today . . . every decision that I've ever made in my entire life has been wrong. My life is the complete opposite of every-thing I want it to be. Every instinct I have in every aspect of life, be it something to wear, something to eat . . . it's all been wrong. Every one.

WAITRESS: (pointing at George) Tuna on toast, coleslaw, cup of coffee.

GEORGE: Yeah. No, no, wait a minute! I always have tuna on toast. Nothing's ever worked out for me with tuna on toast. I want the complete opposite of tuna on toast. (Becomes excited) Chicken salad. On rye. Untoasted. With a side of potato salad, and a cup of tea . . . ha ha!

ELAINE: Well, there's no telling what can happen from this.

JERRY: Yeah, chicken salad's not the opposite of tuna. Salmon's the opposite of tuna because salmon swim against the current and the tuna swim with it.

GEORGE: (Sarcastically) Good for the tuna.

ELAINE: George, you know that woman just looked at you.

GEORGE: So what? What am I supposed to do?

ELAINE: Go talk to her.

GEORGE: Elaine, bald men with no jobs, and no money, who live with their parents, don't approach strange women.

JERRY: Well here's your chance to try the opposite. Instead of tuna salad and being intimidated by women, chicken salad and going right up to her.

GEORGE: Yeah, I should do the opposite! I should!

JERRY: If every instinct you have is wrong, then the opposite would have to be right.

GEORGE: (Triumphantly) Yes, I will do the opposite! I used to sit here and do nothing and regret it the rest of the day. So now I will do the opposite and I will do something! (Gets up and approaches woman) Excuse me, ah, I couldn't help but notice that you were looking in my direction.

WOMAN: Oh, yes, I was. You just ordered the same exact lunch as me.

GEORGE: (Pauses, then defiantly) My name is George. I am unemployed and I live with my parents.

WOMAN: (Smiles with obvious interest) I'm Victoria. Hi!

Later in the episode, as his fortunes multiply due to this new method of decision-making, George says to Jerry:

This has been the dream of my life, ever since I was a child. And it's all happening because I am completely ignoring every urge towards common sense and good judgment I've ever had! This is no longer some crazy notion. Elaine, Jerry: This is my religion!

We see here just one example (and the remainder of the episode provides dozens more) of one of Aristotle's chief contentions: that you just can't trust a washout like George when it comes to valuing, let alone acting. Aristotle writes:

> But the many disagree about what happiness is, and the many do not give the same answer as the wise. For the many think it is something obvious and evident, such as pleasure, wealth or honor, some thinking one thing, others another; and indeed the same person keeps changing his mind, since in sickness he thinks it is health, in poverty wealth. And when they are conscious of their own ignorance, they admire anyone who speaks of something grand and beyond them. (1095a25)

This is virtually a primer of George's life, and the dialogue from "The Opposite" illustrates well the two main flaws in George's character. First, his reasoning skills are terrible (although to be fair, he was egged on by Jerry, so perhaps George is merely stupid), and second, as one might expect in a person with whom reason has taken a backseat, George's emotions affect his life much in the way Aristotle predicts, as we shall see.

Aristotle and George are polar opposites because they think about what man seeks in life in a completely different way. Aristotle rejects the widespread belief that value judgments are a special kind of judgment. Contemporary philosophers commonly think of value judgments as either (1) not judgments of fact, or (2) judgments of a kind of facts that are quite different from the facts involved in judgments of the physical world. The good, for Aristotle, is whatever man, in virtue of his nature, is actually seeking. What does man seek? Unfortunately, there is no single English word that captures the meaning of Aristotle's term, *eudaimonia*. It will be sufficient for our purposes, however, to adopt the most common explanation, which is that the good for man is the fulfillment of his function. But what is his function? (Aristotle himself expresses it as "the actuality of the soul with respect to its function" [1098a16].) Aristotle writes:

> What, then, could this [function] be? For living is apparently shared with plants, but what we are looking for is the special function of a human being; hence we should set aside the life of nutrition and

growth. The life next in order is some sort of life of sense perception; but this too is apparently shared, with horse, ox, and every animal. The remaining possibility, then, is some sort of life of action of the part of the soul that has reason. (1098a)

And shortly:

The excellent man's function is to [engage in actions that express reason] finely and well . . . The human good turns out to be the soul's activity that expresses virtue. (1098a15)

The rational control of desires is the province of moral virtue. Moral virtue is fostered through continuous practice (which produces habit). Aristotle writes:

A state of character arises from the repetition of similar activities. Hence we must display the right activities, since differences in these imply corresponding differences in the states. It is not unimportant, then, to acquire one sort of habit or another, right from our youth; rather, it is very important, indeed, all-important. (1103b25)

But moral virtue itself is constituted by action that is a mean between two extremes. Aristotle further writes:

Virtue, then, is (a) a state that decides, (b) consisting in a mean, (c) the mean relative to us, (d) which is defined by reference to reason, . . . It is a mean between two vices, one of excess and one of deficiency. (1107a)

But—and this is a big "but" for George—action is not virtuous *because* it represents a mean between two extremes (both of which are vices); rather, it is virtuous because it is performed in conformity with reason, and it represents a mean as a consequence. Aristotle writes: "First, then, actions should express correct reason" (1103b30).

Living well in the way just described is the ultimate end for man (including George, as hard as it may be to believe). But this end is not a matter of choice for man; it is his nature to have a life of reason as constituting the good life. George, of course, is so far from living the good life that a life of reason might seem to him bizarre. (I shall develop this point in the next section.) In this paper, I suggest that George will never be happy; that we have no reason to believe that he will adopt a life of reason and thus moderation.

Why George is a Virtueless Man (In Twentieth Centuryspeak: Why George is a Pathetic Slob)

George's personality might seem at first blush to be a single-handed refutation of Aristotle's claim that man is the highest creation, a being who in some way partakes of that which is divine in the universe. Although man is of nature, a creature containing matter, he is also of the divine. Man is not necessarily lost in the *pot-pourri* of the material universe, and is able to approach the divine because he is of the same nature as the divine. This claim seems hard to believe when George is used as the standard.

The distinguishing feature of man is his reason, and Aristotle believed that the highest good of man is the complete realization of his reason. This, Aristotle believed, brings happiness. But, both Plato and Aristotle agree, reason is only one of the parts of man. He also has feelings, desires, and appetites. This means that a good life is one in which all the facets of man achieve a certain harmony, in which reason rules and feelings and desires play a subservient role. This rule of reason, which elevates reason but does not ignore emotion, Aristotle claims consists of the "Golden Mean." For example, courage is the mean between cowardice and foolhardiness. The good man is one whose actions fall somewhere between two extremes. For Aristotle, the definition of happiness or the good life is activity in accordance with virtue, and thus is the harmonious fulfillment of man's natural tendencies.

George cannot hope to even approximate this ideal. Why? In the first place, George *hates himself.* In "The Outing," George sums up his attitude toward himself, explaining to a girlfriend:

> You can do better than me. You could throw a dart out the window and hit someone better than me. I'm no good!

He hates his body:

I always get the feeling that when lesbians look at me, they're thinking, "That's why I'm not a heterosexual." ("The Subway")

He hates his personality:

I am so psychosomatic it makes me sick just thinking about it!

I'm disturbed! I'm depressed! I'm inadequate! I got it all!! ("The Visa")

He hates his inability to interact with women:

When I like them, they don't like me, when they like me, I don't like them. Why can't I act with the ones I like the same way I do with the ones I don't like? ("The Old Man")

For me to ask a woman out, I've got to get into a mental state like the karate guys before they break the bricks. ("The Phone Message")

He hates that he is weak-willed:

Yeah, I'm a great quitter. It's one of the few things I do well. I come from a long line of quitters. My father was a quitter, my grandfather was a quitter . . . I was raised to give up. ("The Old Man")

Conformity's an obsession with me. ("The Pie")

He hates that his life is boring:

Because if I watch [a video] at my apartment I feel like I'm not doing anything. If I watch it here, I'm out of the house; I'm doing something. ("The Junior Mints")

Worst of all, he hates that his faults are obvious, especially to the opposite sex:

When women smile at me I don't know what it means. Sometimes I interpret it like they're psychotic or something. ("The Phone Message")

She thinks I'm a nice guy. Women always think I'm nice. But women don't want nice. ("The Cafe")

I have no power. Why should she have the upper hand? Once in my life I would like the upper hand. I have no hand. No hand at all. She has the hand. I have no hand. ("The Pez Dispenser")

What do these quotations have in common besides demonstrating George's hatred of himself? They indicate the *way* in which George regards his shortcomings. George believes that his lot in life is a matter of fortune. He rarely takes responsibility for what happens to him, and he looks to others to improve his station in life. We see this, for example, when George proclaims that "It's a different world when you're with a cool guy" ("The Stall") (thinking that his life can be improved not by him, but by the presence of someone cool), and the negative manifestation of this same phenomenon when George fears the presence of Jerry at a crucial moment: "Would it kill you not to be so funny all the time? That's all I'm askin'. This woman thinks I'm very funny and now you're gonna be funny, so what am I gonna be? I'm gonna be a short bald guy with glasses who suddenly doesn't seem so funny" ("The Visa"). But once again we find him at odds with Aristotle, who writes: "We have said that [happiness] is a certain sort of activity of the soul expressing virtue, (and hence not a product of fortune)" (1099b25).

George's Brushes with Happiness

George essentially encounters two kinds of experiences that *he* would characterize as happiness. First, he experiences momentary elation, typically when he has achieved some victory over others. Often, he expresses this victory in terms of attaining something that he has always wanted, but the desirability of the thing attained is almost always dependent on George's perception that others receive the very thing that until now has been denied to him. For example, in "The Parking Spot," George argues: "My father didn't pay for parking, my mother, my brother, nobody. It's like going to a prostitute. Why should I pay for it? If I apply myself, maybe I can get it for free." Were George actually to *get* the free parking, he would doubtless erupt in a sort of paroxysm of joy, proclaiming to Jerry what a magnificent *victory* had been won. This is George's way: to see himself in the context of others; to adopt a sort of scarcity mentality where there is never enough to go around and there must always be a loser (usually him). By transforming others into losers, he erroneously believes that he is thus transformed into a winner; that he is what he is only by comparison to others. Whether called approval-seeking, other-directed, or reactive behavior, such conduct is not uncommon. George, however, is a caricature of a man who measures himself by measuring himself against others.

In such cases, however, we do not have to have read Aristotle to see that George is not happy. Although it is true that George may feel some momentary elation, any *Seinfeld* devotee knows that for George, his elation is never more than momentary. Why? Because George's personality will always intervene eventually. As we saw earlier, for Aristotle the definition of happiness or the good life is activity in accordance with virtue, and thus as the harmonious fulfillment of man's natural tendencies. How does George's personality intervene? For example, George explains that "I cannot express to you the feeling I get from a perfect airport pickup" ("The Airport"). We know of course, that whatever enjoyment George gets from something this simple and transient will immediately be overridden by something else (equally insignificant) that will douse his happiness and replace it with (pick one: fury, ardor, frustration, insecurity, or something else). But like everyone, George knows that his life is lacking; he sees that he is at the mercy of his seesawing passions. But lacking the skills to deal with this problem, his attempts to solve it are merely examples of surrender: George asks, "Why can't I just exist?" and "I don't want hope. Hope is killing me. My dream is to become hopeless. When you're hopeless you don't care. And when you don't care, that indifference makes you attractive" ("The Fix-Up").

Surely no one can doubt that George recognizes that he is pathetic. George himself learns that the best he can hope for is that others will recognize the deficiencies of his personality and feel benevolence; as he says in "The Busboy" episode: "Pity's very underrated. I like pity. It's good." George sees that pity is the only emotion that he will elicit from others that may benefit him. But if George knows that his life is lacking, why doesn't he improve? Leaving aside the financial reasons for the producers of the show, we can consider George in the abstract. Let us assume for our purposes that George is a real person (perhaps we all know a George) and ask, Can George become virtuous?

George and Virtue—Like Oil and Water

George is doomed. I don't say this just because he is a pathetic slob with a scarcity mentality who hates women and has zero self-esteem. The real reason why George is doomed is because we have seen him for eight years, and George is no closer to happiness at the end than in the beginning. Rather, he continues to manifest the same lack of virtue that makes him a popular character (popular probably because he is so wretched that we feel reassured about ourselves). But can we be certain that George will not change?

Predicting a person's future is difficult; but predicting George's seems less difficult than others. Will he become virtuous? One way to decide whether he will adopt a more Aristotelian perspective is to consider Aristotle's suggestions for achieving a virtuous mean in our actions. In 1109a20–1109b10, Aristotle describes three ways to encourage virtuous action. Are these methods ones that George is likely to adopt? Let us consider them:

1. *Avoid the more opposed extreme.* Aristotle writes: "Hence if we aim at the intermediate condition we must first of all steer clear of the more contrary extreme" (1109a30–31). One of the aims of the dialogue first quoted, in which George decides to adopt an irresponsible, devil-may-care attitude toward every facet of his life, is to show that George is completely willing to embrace the more extreme of the two extremes of conduct. In addition, we know from other episodes that George is prone to sadism (see the final episode), miserliness (see "The Parking Spot"), and rage (see any episode).

2. *Avoid the easier extreme.* Aristotle writes:

> We must also examine what we ourselves drift into easily. For different people have different natural tendencies toward goals, and we shall come to know our own tendencies from the pleasure or pain that arises in us. We must drag ourselves off in the contrary direction. (1109b1–4)

Save the passage quoted at the outset, George does not fight his inclinations, nor do we sense that he has the strength to do so. For example, if there is anything that is a hallmark of the way George conducts himself, it is his laziness. George spent entire seasons unemployed, and when he did get work, he usually didn't do any actual *work*. Can we really believe that this will change?

3. *Be careful with pleasures.* Aristotle writes:

> And in everything we must beware above all of pleasure and its sources; for we are already biased in its favor when we come to judge it. (1109b8–9)

George is not alone in his pleasure seeking; a common theme among the show's characters is the pursuit of pleasure, even if at the expense of others. In this regard we have perhaps the rule which is least likely to be followed: not only is George himself inclined to seek pleasure, but those around him do so as well, and it is of course our nature to do so excessively.

If we agree that George is not virtueless, and that it is unlikely that he will become virtuous, perhaps we ought to ask ourselves the question, Can George become virtuous? Is virtue even possible for George? Aristotle discusses this problem. He writes:

> However, someone might raise this puzzle: 'What do you mean by saying that to become just we must first do just actions and to become temperate we must first do temperate actions? For if we do what is grammatical or musical, we must already be grammarians or musicians. In the same way, then, if we do what is just or temperate, we must already be just or temperate. (1105a20)

Aristotle thinks that this analogy is a poor one. He points out that we might produce something grammatical by chance or by following someone else's directions. But further:

> [A]ctions are called just or temperate when they are the sort that a just or temperate person would do. But the just or temperate person is not the one who merely does these actions, but the one who also does them in the way in which just or temperate people do them. It is right, then, to say that a person comes to be just from doing just actions and temperate from doing temperate actions." (1105b5–10)

So it seems there may be hope for George. I don't think there is very much hope, however. While it is true that George may begin to act virtuously (God knows why he would do this), and continue to act virtuously so often that acting virtuously becomes a habit (we couldn't even look to God for help in understanding that one), then, and only then, might George's life improve. But since the chances of George habitually acting virtuously are about the same as Jerry learning to live with head lice, we can safely say that George's miserable existence shall continue (fortunately for us).

3
Elaine Benes: Feminist Icon or Just One of the Boys?

SARAH E. WORTH

"The negation of aesthetic, spiritual, and moral values has become an ethics; unruliness has become a rule." (Motto for *Seinfeld* writers?)

—Simone de Beauvoir, *The Ethics of Ambiguity*

Popular culture shapes the way we think about the world and about ourselves. Television especially has an influence on us because it is so easily accessible—it arrives in our private living space. Often, we are not even aware of the impact television can have. Thus, in shaping the morality of the characters it portrays, TV has a tremendous impact on how we perceive the world. Women especially are susceptible to the stereotypes presented through television. As the average female television character falls into a certain set of stereotypes, we presume that those stereotypes should work in the real world as well. Elaine Benes, on the other hand, defies many of the media stereotypes of thirty-something women on television. Though she defies these stereotypes, her moral character is not necessarily one to emulate. In this essay we shall examine the structure of Elaine's moral character and ask how well she fits the role of a Nineties feminist icon.

Is She a Feminist?

Could Elaine possibly be a feminist? This, of course, depends on one's definition of feminism. Liberal feminism is derived from the notion of liberty, that is, the right of each individual to behave as she or he wishes, legitimately limited only by the requirement not to interfere with others. Liberal feminism then aims at "the achievement of equal opportunity between women and men: in education, in access to career opportunities, in compensation and advancement. Liberal feminists also strive to ensure women and men equal treatment under law, equal advantage under legislation and taxation, and equal opportunity for self-determination."[1] In comparison with her *Seinfeld*ian cohorts, Elaine does pretty well in all these areas, though this alone does not necessarily make her a feminist. In terms of education, Elaine is the only one with a degree from a highly selective college, Tufts University (which, in fact, she claims was her "safety school"). Both Jerry and George went to the less selective Queens College. She also seems to be the only one who works in a field that would require such an education, at least while she is at the publishing company. In terms of career opportunities, Elaine seems to win in this arena as well, in comparison to her three friends. She is the only one who has a steady job through the whole series. She spends her nine seasons at Pendant Publishing, the J. Peterman Catalogue, and doing a short stint working in a dead end job for Mr. Pitt. No one knows where Kramer makes his money, although he is always involved in some sort of monetary scheme. Jerry has always had a steady job as a comic, but one wonders how long that might really last as the work is always sporadic. (At one point, both his parents and Kramer urge him to take a look at the Bloomingdales executive training program!) Everyone knows that George is unable to hold a job.

Nor is Elaine different with respect to treatment under the law. The last episode made abundantly clear that Elaine was as immoral as the rest (perhaps even more immoral, being the only one to sleep with the attorney!), and was not tried any differently. She would be expected to serve time just like the

---

1 Eve Browning Cole, *Philosophy and Feminist Criticism: An Introduction* (New York: Paragon House, 1993), p. 6.

others, perhaps even in the same prison, so the four would not be separated.

Elaine has plenty of self-determination. She is not obsessed with her career, but is self-centered, as are her friends. She looks for advantages for herself and if the others benefit as well, then great. If not, she still looks out for herself, especially in terms of her relations with her barrage of boyfriends. In essence, Elaine would seem to have achieved all the aims of a liberal feminist agenda, but this is not necessarily enough to qualify her as a feminist. Being the smartest one of the bunch and the only one who can keep a job does not make her a feminist. For *Seinfeld,* it just makes her one of the boys. Cast as Jerry's ex-girlfriend, she ended up being an anti-girlfriend—a good friend whom Jerry can treat like he treats his other male friends. Being one of the boys, however, does not a feminist make.

Elaine and Feminist Ethics

Although Elaine may not be a feminist, she is perhaps the most independent of the four main characters. She has clearly been affected by the fact that feminism is a powerful force in society. She does not fight for the cause *per se,* but she is not dependent on men financially or emotionally. She keeps a steady job and lives an independent life. What about her ethical status though? Does she practice feminist ethics even though she isn't a feminist? One of the most popular brands of feminist ethics is the ethic of care (feminine), which is generally seen in opposition to an ethic of justice (masculine). This distinction was originally made in the work of Carol Gilligan,[2] working in response to psychologist Lawrence Kohlberg's moral development theory. In the 1960s Kohlberg devised a series of tests which were said to measure the "moral maturity" of his subjects. There were six levels, the sixth being "moral sainthood." Kohlberg's model of moral maturity was derived from Immanuel Kant's ideal which claimed as attributes the avoidance of emotional grounds for moral action, a disposition to think of ethics in terms of justice and laws, and the capacity for self-sacrificing behavior on behalf of humanity. Moral sainthood at level six is reserved only for

---

2 Carol Gilligan, *In a Different Voice: Psychological Theory and Women's Development* (Cambridge: Harvard University Press, 1982).

those who devote their whole lives to the welfare of others. As one might guess, men scored consistently higher on this moral maturity test (although it is unlikely that Jerry, George, or Kramer would do so much better than Elaine—all of them would be stuck at the basement level).

Gilligan decided to do some testing of her own to see if the paradigm of moral maturity for women was different from that for men. It seemed unlikely to her that men, in general, were more morally developed. She came to the conclusion that women do, indeed, have a different moral structure. First, she claimed that in reasoning through a specific moral dilemma women tend to focus on specific relationships between people rather than only on the justice or fairness of the situation. Women are concerned with how the people involved will be affected. Secondly, women think that relationships entail certain responsibilities, and that these responsibilities are very specific within each relationship. Thus there is an emphasis on the particularity of the relationship involved—as every relationship is different and should be considered to be so.

Following Gilligan's work in feminist ethics, Nel Noddings developed a slightly different approach based on care.[3] This is also based on the ethical situations of caring for appropriate individuals. The central directive of an ethic of care is that "I should act always in such ways as to promote the well-being of both the others to whom I am in relation and the self which is relationally constituted."[4] This is obviously vague, but it is this way purposely, so that one has the flexibility to consider different situations and different people. How does this relate to Elaine Benes? She is not a paragon of care. She seems to care for her three friends in the show, but as Julia Louis-Dreyfus claimed in an interview with *People Magazine,* the three friends are "there for one another, but they usually let one another down."[5] Certainly they care for one another, but they generally all care for themselves more. One might expect that Elaine, as the late feminine addition to the cast, would have some consistent caring feminine influence, but, in fact,

---

[3] Nel Noddings, *Caring: A Feminine Approach to Moral Education.* (Berkeley: University of California Press, 1984).

[4] Cole, p. 107.

[5] *People Magazine: Special Seinfeld Farewell Issue* (Spring 1998), pp. 12–14

Elaine's estrogen does not bring much compassion to the show. She may even be seen as less caring than the men just because she defies this stereotypical role. By being one of the boys, she leaves her femininity and her ethic of care at the door.

Not only does Elaine not particularly care about her three close friends, she doesn't care about the men she dates either. Elaine always seems to be dating someone, but her boyfriends rarely last more than one or two episodes. She is fickle, breaking up with men for petty reasons, refusing to care about them for any length of time. Her family is rarely mentioned, and when they are, it is not in a particularly caring light. There is some mention of Elaine's father, Alton Benes, a Hemingway like figure ("The Jacket"). He is a hard-drinking famous author who appears in only one episode (whereas both Jerry and George's parents appear constantly—even though both relationships are strained, the families are still present). Elaine's father makes her nervous, and also doesn't think much of her friends (he thinks George is gay and Jerry is funny, but effeminate). Elaine has a sister named Gail who lives in St. Louis, but they do not get along and she is scarcely mentioned. As before, her self-centeredness deters her from having any truly caring relationships.

Maternal ethics, a spin-off of care ethics, claims that there is no essential connection between being a "mother" (someone who does maternal work) and being a woman. Men can do maternal work, and women can refuse it, but generally, based on the caring ethics of women, they often do the mothering. But Elaine has none of this maternal instinct either. Elaine wants nothing to do with motherhood, but when her friend Vivian (who is sick) chooses someone else to baby-sit, Elaine resents this decision. She says, "I couldn't raise a kid? But I love bossing people around!" This seems to be the extent of her maternal instinct. She is also offended when an attractive pediatrician calls both Elaine and what she thinks is an ugly baby "breathtaking" ("The Hamptons"). She has no feeling for an unattractive baby—doesn't even want to hold it, and she cannot stop thinking of herself long enough to give a thought to a child. On the other hand, she cannot resist the attractive physician! This woman is not a good candidate for motherhood or for care ethics in general.

One day Elaine's secret comes out. She desperately wants to get married. In "The Engagement," when George announces his engagement to Susan, Elaine is secretly jealous. She will not admit it to either Jerry or George, but talks to Rabbi Kirschbaum, who lives in her building. She admits, "for some reason I feel myself just overcome with feelings of jealousy and resentment." The Rabbi asks if she feels any joy for her friend whatsoever and she explains that the whole thing just makes her sick. She feels no happiness for George, just a feeling that *she* should be the one getting married. As she explains further, "it should have been *me. I'm* smart. *I'm* attractive." Thus she implies that since George is neither of these things, he should not get married first. Elaine has plenty of men to date, but she refuses to get serious with any of them, so it would seem logical that she might never even manage to get engaged. Let us look further into Elaine's dating ethics in order to find out more about her moral character, or the morality of her character as the case may be.

Elaine's Dating Ethics

Though there is not a set philosophical corpus on dating ethics *per se*, there are still some standard rules of conduct that might be applied in the case of Elaine's dating life. It is well known that her love life is a disaster. She dates one loser after another, rarely keeping a boyfriend for more than one show. But she seems to have pretty high standards for keeping them. Perhaps they are too high. As explained above, in an apparent moment of weakness, she claims that she is desperate to get married. She wouldn't admit this to her friends, but it seems to be her secret wish. She also seems to have no problem finding men to date— although they don't last more than one episode, there is usually at least one *in* every episode. It is also interesting to note that she is willing to put up with all sorts of things with her *Seinfeldian* cohorts that she would not put up with in a man she was dating. She is always (relatively) nice to Jerry, George, and Kramer, even when they are not getting along or when they have minor disputes. But minor disputes with boyfriends are unacceptable, and she will not hesitate to break off a relationship.

Elaine is very fickle when it comes to men. This is not news. She has had numerous boyfriends and love interests throughout the nine seasons, including, but not limited to, Aaron (the close talker), Lloyd Braun ("A BIG Advisor to Mayor Dinkins"), Joel Rifkin (not the serial killer), Tim Whatley (the dentist), Jake Jarmel, her therapist, a "hot and heavy" musician, NBC executive Russell Dalrymple, the "maestro," baseball's Keith Hernandez, a pediatrician, a dim-witted near-doctor, a 66-year-old-writer, a physician who taught her about tongue hygiene, an Eagles-loving "Desperado," a teenage film aficionado, "The Wiz," and David Puddy (a mechanic turned car salesman, who actually lasted more than one show). All of these men were attractive (she wouldn't even bother if they weren't), but none seemed to have everything she was looking for in a long-term relationship. She claims once to have broken up with a guy because he didn't *offer* her pie. She broke up with someone else because his bathroom wasn't clean and another because he didn't agree with a woman's right to choose to have an abortion. She broke up with Puddy, in the middle of a car sale to Jerry, because he had the annoying habit of wanting to "high five" people all the time. In "The Reverse Peephole" Puddy wears a fur coat. Elaine at one time had some moral issues with fur ("but who has the energy anymore?"), but now is more concerned about being seen "hanging on the arm of an idiot."

Elaine is open with regard to whom she will date (as long as he is attractive). Her ethics in this area are, however, questionable. In "The Strongbox" she is willing to date a man she thinks is married, with some moral questioning of herself, but once she finds out he is actually poor (thus all of his secrecy) she wants to dump him. She then, of course, finds out that he is married *and* poor. In "The Wait Out" she has designs on another married man (while Jerry waits for the man's wife), whose marriage is on the rocks. She allows herself to date an intern, even though he isn't a *real* doctor. At one point, she even thinks she can "convert" a gay man, "get him to switch teams."

There is also an entire show dedicated to Elaine and her preferred method of birth control—the sponge. When she finds out that the "Today Sponge" is going off the market completely she goes to all of the drug stores within a 25-block radius to buy as many as she can. Eventually she finds a store with a whole case left, which she buys, sheepishly. She then decides that she has to raise the standards by which she judges men. She resolves to determine whether the men are "spongeworthy" before she will have sex with them. As she was attempting to decide with her man of the week, she asked him to run down his qualifications for her again. One of the qualifications that he cited was a clean bathroom. Indeed, he cleaned his bathroom because she forced him to do it in order to be deemed spongeworthy! Once he convinced her that he was, actually, spongeworthy, he was told in no uncertain terms the next morning that it was good, but definitely not worth two!

Elaine has not always been faithful to the sponge though. In a "must see" masturbatory episode, "The Contest," she mentions to Jerry's girl of the week, Marla (Jane Leeves, now Daphne on *Frasier*) that her diaphragm flew out of her purse at a party. Marla, who has just divulged to Jerry that she is a virgin, is horrified. Elaine goes on and on about how normal it is for a woman to carry a diaphragm around with her at all times, since one never knows when one might need it. Marla continues to be horrified as Elaine leads her to think that she is much more promiscuous than she really is. Or not.

When she has a boyfriend, Elaine is happy. When she has a boyfriend but she is not having sex, she turns stupid. In "The Abstinence" George becomes brilliant and even temporarily loses interest in sex when forced to abstain from it. Observing this, Elaine and her *beau du jour* abstain from sex with the hope that he will finally pass his medical licensing exams. He too becomes brilliant and passes his exam, while she becomes as dumb as a stump. Evidently, not all things affect the sexes in the same way!

Although Elaine was not a part of the original show, *The Seinfeld Chronicles*, she was quickly written in as Jerry's ex-girlfriend. For the most part there is not even sexual tension between the two, but at one point while Jerry and Elaine are sitting on the couch, bored, they decide it would be a good idea to have sex—since it had been a while for both of them. Before engaging in "the act," however, they make three rules, so as not to destroy the friendship (this) but still be able to have sex (that) without having to develop a romantic involvement (the other). The agreed upon rules are that 1. no one has to call the next day, 2. spending the night is optional, and 3. the goodnight kiss is optional. They are confident that, although no one has ever been able to have casual sex while not affecting the friendship, with these rules they can do it. As it turns out, however, unlike her usual fickle self, Elaine is the one who cannot deal with the arrangements. She wants it all—she wants this, that, and the other! It seems that Elaine is running a bit of a double standard when it comes to men. What she demands of men, what she asks of Jerry, and what she really seems to want are three totally different things. Elaine also accepts Jerry's marriage proposal in "The Serenity Now" after he breaks up with Patti (Lori Laughlin). He becomes an emotional basketcase, telling everyone (George and Kramer included) that he loves them. But Jerry eventually comes back to his old self, and rescinds his offer of marriage to Elaine.

This is not to say that this call for a double standard is a character flaw for Elaine. It could be an ingenious bit of writing for her character. As noted above, Elaine was not originally written into the pilot, *The Seinfeld Chronicles,* but she was added later, when the folks at NBC thought it unlikely that a show with just three men could be a hit. Seinfeld claimed that the show "lacked estrogen."[6] Rather than writing Elaine in as a girlfriend, they added her only as an ex-girlfriend (of which there seem to be dozens). She had a history with Jerry, but both were then free to have dating lives separate from each other—something essential to the show's survival.

Elaine's Moral Character

Elaine is an independent woman in ways that many other media women are not. As explained above, she defies the feminine stereotypes. She is not ultra-thin or obsessed with her weight (and in fact Louis-Dreyfus went through two pregnancies without anyone noticing). She is not emotionally dependent on a man to keep her happy all the time, but she and her friends do seem to keep each other going. Importantly, I think, she is not financially dependent on anyone. As mentioned above, she is the only one who seems to be able to hold a steady job. She is also not particularly vain. She doesn't look in the mirror constantly (although she is convinced at one point that a store mannequin is modeled after her) and she hates the famed chick flick, *The English Patient.*

---

[6] Greg Gattuso, *Seinfeld Universe: The Entire Domain* (Secaucus: Citadel Press, 1996), p. 136

It is clear, however, that although this is a show about nothing in particular, it is also a show about how men and women relate to each other. Elaine isn't originally in the pilot for *Jerry* (also a show about nothing) that Seinfeld and Costanza pitch to NBC because they claim that they can't write for a woman. They don't know what a woman would say. This clearly indicates the gap between the sexes (on the other hand, they don't have much luck writing for themselves either). But Elaine and Jerry never seem to be at a loss for words in Jerry's apartment, or at Monk's.

Elaine has no close female friends. They do show up here and there—Vivian, who wants Elaine to be the guardian of her child, the friend on Long Island who gives birth to the ugly baby in "The Hamptons," and, of course, Sue Ellen Mishki. Kramer once comments to Elaine that she is a "man's woman—you hate other women and they hate you." She thus attempts to befriend George's fiancée, Susan, which seems to work until George's two worlds (friend world and girlfriend world) collide and cause George to have a panic attack—almost killing *independent George!*

One might wonder why this reasonably successful, attractive, and funny woman would choose to hang out with these three particular men. In "The Bizarro Jerry" Elaine does adopt a new set of friends. They are exactly the opposite of her three existing friends. They eat at Reggie's Diner, they like to read, and Feldman (the Kramer Opposite) always politely knocks before entering a room. She embraces them, but they dump her, claiming that her manner is too rough. She helps herself to the fridge, and uses her "get out!" and famous push, which is a bit too much for them to handle. Thus she remains loyal to Jerry, George, and Kramer.

Being billed as one of the boys, Elaine is still able to portray many positive feminist traits that some of the other Thursday night Must See TV women do not embrace. The women she shared the evening with are not quite the role models that Elaine is. In just the recent past, the women on *Friends* are not women one would want to emulate (aside from Jennifer Aniston's haircut, which was all the rage). None of these women have stable careers. Although Monica seems to be a competent chef, she cannot find a steady job. Rachel only recently made the transition from coffeehouse waitress to fashion executive (unlikely even in fiction), and Phoebe plays her guitar for money on the streets. None of them are especially well-educated, and Phoebe in particular is quite the dumb blonde. All three are, of course, attractive, vain and model thin.

Of the two women on *Frasier*, Daphne and Roz, both are thin and attractive. But Daphne is a live-in healthcare worker *cum* baby-sitter for Frasier's father (and thrilled to do it) with little social life of her own, and Roz has a steady career but cannot find love. When *Cheers* shared the night with *Seinfeld*, there were three other stereotypical women. Carla was stable, but bitchy and unattractive. Diane and Rebecca were both attractive but high strung and emotionally unstable in their own ways. The most recent addition to Must See TV was *Veronica's Closet*, which stars two heavier women, one of whom owns her own business. This seems to be a step in the right direction perhaps, but they work in the beauty (sex) industry, thus implying that this is the only kind of business a woman could run.

None of these women come close to the ideal that Elaine sets for the impressionable viewer. She is strong and independent but still enjoys the company of men (lots of men). She can maintain friendships with men (something which can be difficult for single women to do as adults), and she doesn't let others push her around. On the other hand, she lies and cheats; she can be rude, vain, inconsiderate, and unreasonable. These problems aside, she is not strong enough to claim to be a feminist, although she seems to have feminist tendencies and is definitely a product of feminism (having these negative qualities would not necessarily prohibit one from being a feminist). She is still too concerned with what others will think of her to be as strong as she might be. The concern among women today that people (men especially) will perceive them as feminists (read man-hating lesbians) is widespread. Women like Elaine can help the media take steps toward presenting independent women to the public, women who can have lives of their own and still include men in their lives as well. If the men can't handle it, then they can just GET OUT!

4
Kramer and Kierkegaard: Stages on Life's Way

WILLIAM IRWIN

The Danish philosopher Søren Kierkegaard (1813–1855) was a forerunner of existentialism and has undoubtedly been a tremendous influence on much twentieth-century Continental philosophy. The American sitcom character Cosmo Kramer (1989–1998) has certainly made millions laugh, but his philosophical significance is not immediately apparent. The purpose of this essay is, in part, to highlight that significance. To do so we shall explore Kierkegaard's philosophy, taking Kramer as our guide.

Perhaps Kierkegaard's best-known contribution to philosophy is his theory of the three stages of human existence: the aesthetic stage, the ethical stage, and the religious stage. The aesthetic stage is marked by pleasure-seeking and a lack of commitment. It does not necessarily have to do with the beautiful or with the arts, as its name might suggest. The aesthetic stage both begins and ends in despair, leading to the ethical stage, which, in contrast, is marked by commitment. This is the stage at which one commits oneself to the "universal," the stage at which one commits to the values of society. With the loss of individuality, which often characterizes the ethical stage, one may then move on to the religious stage. The religious stage is paradoxical; in it the individual becomes higher than the universal. One moves beyond the "universal" values of society and discovers an absolute duty to God. Kierkegaard describes the religious stage by reflecting on the biblical story in which Abraham is willing to break the universal prohibition against murder by taking the life of his only begotten son, Isaac. In this story, Abraham, an individual, becomes higher than the universal moral law in discovering his absolute duty to God.

These "stages on life's way" can also be described as "spheres of existence."[1] They are not necessary steps that each individual must take through the course of his or her own development. Rather, they describe certain modes or spheres of existence, certain ways of living and believing. Kierkegaard himself did indeed move through each of the three stages, but this does not suggest that he thought everyone did. We should also note that movement from one stage to the next is not easy, but may actually require a leap of faith.

What, then, does any of this have to do with *Seinfeld?* A fair question. I suggest that the character Kramer provides us with an excellent example of someone dwelling in the aesthetic sphere of existence. Kramer is constantly in pursuit of what he finds interesting and pleasurable, and, of course, what he finds interesting and pleasurable is constantly changing. To a certain degree this may be said of Jerry, George, and Elaine as well, but, as we shall see, Kramer is the aesthete *par excellence.*

In this essay, then, we shall shed light on Kierkegaard's stages on life's way through an examination of Kramer, "The K man." Accordingly, we shall focus primarily on the aesthetic stage. In closing the essay, however, we shall perform a thought experiment by imagining what it would be like for the K man to move to the ethical stage and to the religious stage.

Kramer, Despair, and the Aesthetic Stage

Kierkegaard tells us that the aesthetic stage both begins and ends in despair, and indeed this was true in his own life. Young Søren had been a quiet, melancholy, and religious boy, who revered his father, a man he took to be the paradigm of religious piety. Shortly before Kierkegaard enrolled in the University of Copenhagen his father revealed two terrible secrets to him. The first secret was that when he was a poor boy working as a ser-

---

[1] Merold Westphal, "Kierkegaard," in Simon Critchley and William R. Schroeder eds., *A Companion to Continental Philosophy* (Oxford: Blackwell, 1998), p. 129.

vant on a farm, the elder Kierkegaard had once cursed God for giving him such a miserable lot in life. Although the elder Kierkegaard had gone on to great material prosperity he always felt as if divine retribution were close at hand. The second terrible secret was that the elder Kierkegaard had begun a relationship with his second wife while his first wife was still on her deathbed. He had committed the sin of adultery, and the guilt weighed on his soul. Young Søren reacted strongly to his father's revelations, and was plunged into despair, beginning his own aesthetic stage. Kierkegaard tells of having lived a rowdy existence during his college days, drinking in the bars and engaging in obnoxious behavior. He was without real commitment, seeking pleasure in its various forms.

At the beginning of the series we join the *Seinfeld* crew *in medias res,* in the middle of things. The characters have an important history behind them about which we learn just a little here and there. One important thing we do know about the *Seinfeld* past is that Jerry and Elaine once dated. One important thing we do *not* know is the source of the animosity between Jerry and Newman. (This seems to be more than a case of mutual contempt without reason; there is some history there of which we, the audience, are ignorant.) What do we know about Kramer's past? Exceedingly little. In fact even the other major characters don't seem to know a whole lot about Kramer's history. It is not until the sixth season that they even learn that his first name is Cosmo ("The Switch").[2]

Despite the scarcity of information on Cosmo Kramer's past we do get the occasional hint, and we do know something about him in the present. Kramer, as we shall see, is clearly living in the aesthetic sphere, and this raises the question: What despair led to his aestheticism? The details are sketchy, but we do know that Cosmo Kramer is estranged from his mother, Babs, a boozy ladies' room attendant. It seems safe to assume his father was not around, and that the despair which led to his aestheticism may be related to this.[3] His childhood may not have

---

[2] For the chronological sequence of episode airdates see the Episode Guide at the end of this volume.

[3] Kramer is in possession of his father's wedding band, which in one episode he loans to George so that George can paradoxically attract women by appearing married.

been a happy one, witnessed to by the fact that Kramer is afraid of clowns ("The Gymnast")! We also know that Kramer has a gambling problem, and we may presume that it caused him some trouble in the past since he now abstains (with occasional exceptions) from games of chance. The rush and sense of escape the gambler experiences is much sought after by those who, in truth, are fleeing from themselves. This is likely the case for Kramer who as much as admits to his flight from despair when his first name is finally revealed.

> All my life I've been running away from that name. That's why I wouldn't tell anybody. But I've been thinking about it. All this time I'm trying not to be me. I'm afraid to face who I was. But I'm Cosmo, Jerry, I'm Cosmo Kramer, and that's who I'm going to be. ("The Switch")

Kramer's very appearance suggests some underlying despair. In admiring the portrait of Kramer painted in "The Letter," a rich old husband and wife (though differing with one another) each see into his soul in a way perhaps no one else has.

> "I sense great vulnerability, a man-child crying out for love, an innocent orphan in the postmodern world."
> "I see a parasite, a sexually depraved miscreant who is seeking only to gratify his basest and most immediate urges."
> "His struggle is man's struggle. He lifts my spirit."
> "He is a loathsome, offensive brute—yet I can't look away."
> "He transcends time and space."
> "He sickens me."
> "I love it."
> "Me too." ("The Letter")

They're both right! Kramer embodies the aesthetic stage in its most vulgar form, "seeking only to gratify his basest and most immediate urges," yet we see some part of ourselves in him. His "vulnerability" and flight from despair are common to nearly all.

Kramer, Aestheticism, and "Crop Rotation"

The aesthetic stage begins in despair, and we may at least hypothesize that Kramer's early life was not without its despair.

But what else can we say about the aesthetic stage to tie it to the Kramer we come to know in the show? The aesthetic stage is not only a flight from despair but a flight from boredom as well. If there is one thing the aesthete cannot tolerate it is being bored. Does this sound like anyone you know? Kramer, of course, is never bored. He constantly occupies himself with one pursuit after the next, whether it be a "get rich quick" scheme such as selling raincoats with Morty Seinfeld, a pseudo-athletic endeavor such as swimming in the East River, a fair lady such as the "low talker," or what have you. We shall discuss Kramer's ever-changing pursuits in detail shortly.

Part and parcel of this flight from boredom and despair for the aesthete is an uncanny ability to forget. The aesthete makes an art of forgetting, and this is clearly the case with Kramer. He must forget the failures of his past plans and schemes in order to repeat similar mistakes. The aesthete is inherently selfish, living with the sole concern of what is of interest to him at the moment. His life is experimental and relative; he will pursue a particular pleasure just as long as it is of interest to him. When it ceases to be of interest to him, it ceases to be of value to him, and so it is abandoned. Again, this description fits Kramer like a glove. Kramer puts all his heart into designing a cologne that smells like the beach, or planning a millennium party, or starting up a "make your own pizza" place, but when these things lose their interest to him, he simply abandons them or sticks them on the back of the shelf.

The aesthete never chooses; that is to say, she never chooses with any sense of commitment. She may throw herself entirely into a given endeavor but she will withdraw from it just as entirely. When she becomes bored of it she will leave it behind and forget it. This applies in the realm of values as well. The aesthete is not so much immoral as amoral. She does not choose with commitment any of the values of society; she does not so much reject them as she does fail to take them seriously.[4] To be sure, the aesthete may briefly champion a cause or take a stance, but she will abandon that cause or stance soon enough. Think for example of Kramer's championing of smokers' rights, the Aids walk, his boycott of Kenny Rogers Roasters, *yada yada*

---

[4] Cf. Westphal, p. 130.

yada. The aesthetic Kramer wards off boredom with these fleeting commitments, and never truly faces himself, lost as he is in the spectacle of the moment, of the interest *du jour*.

Kierkegaard presents us with a clear view of the aesthetic stage in his *Either/Or* vol. I.[5] Kierkegaard, we should note, wrote under various pseudonyms so as to distance himself from his work and leave the reader alone with the ideas he presents. *Either/Or* vol. I presents the papers of an aesthete known simply as A. Let's call him "the A man." The papers of the A man are presented as having been edited by Victor Eremita. Kierkegaard, then, should not be taken as advocating the aesthetic stage but simply describing it by means of the character A. Fans of *Seinfeld* are well aware that the K man is no stranger to assuming new identities, most notably H.E. Pennypacker and Dr. Van Nostrand. While Kierkegaard and Kramer clearly have different motivations for concealing their identities (Kierkegaard's motivation is a literary one while Kramer's motivation is usually to deceive someone for his own gain), the parallel is worth noting.

The A man speaks in favor of what he calls the rotation method, a regimen not unlike the crop rotation practiced by farmers. The idea is to constantly vary one's interests and pursuits as well as varying one's very self; the point is to avoid boredom with the same calculation, vigilance, and zeal that a farmer avoids an infertile field. In addition, we should note that there are higher and lower forms of rotation. Let us turn to the words of A for an explanation.

> This is the vulgar inartistic method, and needs to be supported by illusion. One tires of living in the country, and moves to the city; one tires of one's native land, and travels abroad . . . one indulges in a sentimental hope of endless journeyings form star to star. Or the movement is different but still extensive. One tires of porcelain dishes and eats on silver; one tires of silver and turns to gold; one burns half of Rome to get an idea of the burning of Troy. This method defeats itself; it is plain endlessness. (*E/O I*, pp. 287–88)

---

[5] Søren Kierkegaard, *Either/Or* volume I. Trans. David F. Swenson and Lillian Marvin Swenson (Princeton: Princeton University Press, 1959). Further references to this book are indicated in parentheses by *E/O I* accompanied by page numbers.

My method does not consist in change of field, but resembles the
true rotation method in changing the crop and the mode of culti-
vation. Here we have at once the principle of limitation, the only
saving principle in the world. The more you limit yourself, the
more fertile you become in invention. A prisoner in solitary con-
finement for life becomes very inventive, and a spider may furnish
him with much entertainment. One need only hark back to one's
schooldays. We were at an age when aesthetic considerations were
ignored in the choice of one's instructors, most of whom were for
that reason very tiresome; how fertile in invention one then proved
to be! (*E/O I,* p. 288)

Kramer certainly engages in the "vulgar and inartistic" rotation
method often enough. He insists on eating only freshly laid eggs,
or living in the shower, or cutting down on shower time, or wearing only clothes straight out of the dryer, or wearing only jockey
shorts, or wearing no undershorts, or making his own cigars, or
sleeping for only twenty minutes at a time, or storing his own
blood, or reversing his peephole, or slicing his own deli meats.
The list of trivial rotations which Kramer engages in is nearly endless; it is almost constitutive of the very character. But Kramer
does engage in more sophisticated rotation as well. He at times
changes *himself* in his flight from boredom. He thoroughly enjoys
assuming the personae of H.E. Pennypacker and Dr. Van
Nostrand. He also has a passion for acting, varying himself and to
some extent losing himself in the process. In the final episode,
having been sentenced to a year in jail, Kramer is not distressed.
He doesn't think it sounds too bad, and we can rest assured that
he will indeed find ways to amuse himself behind bars.

The A man gives some general prohibitions regarding marriage, work, and friendship which suit the K man well. Let us
first consider what A has to say on the subject of marriage.

One must never enter into the relation of *marriage*. Husband and
wife promise to love one another for eternity. This is all very fine,
but it does not mean very much. . . . If, instead of promising forever, the parties would say: until Easter, or until May-day comes,
there might be some meaning in what they say; for then they
would have said something definite, and also something they might
be able to keep. (*E/O I,* p. 292)

Husband and wife are indeed said to become one, but this is a very
dark and mystic saying. When you are one of several, then you have

lost your freedom; you cannot send for your traveling boots whenever you wish, you cannot move aimlessly about in the world. If you
have a wife it is difficult; if you have a wife and perhaps a child, it
is troublesome; if you have a wife and children, it is impossible. (*E/O
I*, p. 293)

Marriage brings one into fatal connection with custom and tradition, and traditions and customs are like the wind and the weather,
altogether incalculable. (*E/O I*, p. 293)

Clearly the A man sees marriage as a dangerous institution. It
restricts one's freedom, no longer allowing one to follow the
whims of the moment. Constancy, binding oneself to custom
and tradition, is required. Marriage can lead to the death of aestheticism, and so it is to be feared and avoided at all costs.
Compare the words and sentiments of A with those of Kramer
in this lecture to Jerry:

KRAMER: Marriage? Family? They're prisons! Man made prisons! Get up in the morning—she's there. Go to sleep at
night—she's there. You have to ask permission to use the
bathroom! And forget about watching TV while you're
eating because that's DINNER time. And you know what
you do at dinner?

JERRY: What?

KRAMER: You talk about your day. How was your day? Did
you have a good day or a bad day today? I don't know,
what about you? It's sad Jerry. It's a sad state of affairs.

JERRY: I'm glad we had this talk.

KRAMER: Oh, you have no idea. ("The Engagement")

While all the major characters in *Seinfeld* avoid marriage,
none does so as vigorously as Kramer. George and Jerry each
get engaged and Elaine is quite jealous of George's engagement,
but Kramer never even comes close to getting married. For that
matter, Kramer never even has a serious girlfriend.[6] Kramer is
the perennial adolescent, varying himself constantly in his

---

[6] Though in "The Maid," which aired during the final season, some humor
develops around Kramer's girlfriend moving away, "downtown."

romantic pursuits and otherwise. We shall discuss Kramer's romantic pursuits in detail shortly, but for now let us examine the other prohibitions given by the A man.

A also speaks out against committing oneself to work. This too can interfere with one's efforts to vary oneself and remain free.

> One should never accept appointment to an official position. If you do, you will become a mere Richard Roe, a tiny little cog in the machinery of the body politic; you even cease to be a master of your own conduct, and in that case your theories are of little help. You receive a title, and this brings in its train every sin and evil. The law under which you have become a slave is equally tiresome . . . (E/O I, p. 294)

> Even if one abstains from official business, one ought not to be inactive, but should pursue such occupations as are compatible with a sort of leisure; one should engage in all sorts of breadless arts . . . . one should in spite of mature years, be able to prove the truth of the proverb that children are pleased with a rattle and tickled with a straw. (E/O I, p. 294)

Kramer certainly lives up to this aesthetic ideal, never taking on a job which will change his lifestyle. Most of the time, in fact, he does not work at all and has no visible means of support. Let us consider some of the jobs, preoccupations, and "breadless arts" with which Kramer has occupied himself. He has been: the world's oldest ball boy at the U.S. Open, an actor, an underwear model, an author, a bagel maker, a business man, an investor in a non-fat yogurt establishment, a purveyor of raincoats, a movie phone operator, a movie theater restorer, a hansom cab driver, a highway caretaker, the CEO of Kramerica Industries, a seller of personal anecdotes, a rikshaw service owner, a bottle deposit entrepreneur, a shopping mall Santa Claus, a talk show host, and many other things as well. None of these is long lasting. Kramer shows no commitment to any of these ways of earning a living and generally gets out before the obligations become the least bit burdensome. In line with his aestheticism in the area of work, Kramer manifests a political aestheticism as well. Kramer has no allegiance to any organized political party, and indeed has no lasting allegiance to even a political ideology. At one moment he is the champion of capitalism, as in his entrepreneurial endeavors with the Executive Raincoat and non-fat yogurt and in his support of the Mom and Pop dry cleaners. At another moment he and his diminutive pal Mickey are ardent communists ("The Race"). Never does Kramer demonstrate lasting commitment to job or party.

The A man also tells us to beware of friendship. This relationship, like that of marriage, is one which can restrict personal freedom.

> One must guard against *friendship*. How is a friend defined? He is not what philosophy calls the necessary other, but the superfluous third. (*E/O I*, p. 291)

> But because you abstain from friendship it does not follow that you abstain from social contacts. On the contrary, these social relationships may at times be permitted to take on a deeper character, provided you always have so much more momentum in yourself that you can sheer off at will, in spite of sharing for a time in the momentum of the common movement. . . . The essential thing is never to stick fast, and for this it is necessary to have oblivion back of one. The experienced farmer lets his land lie fallow now and then, and the theory of social prudence recommends the same. Everything will doubtless return, though in a different form; that which has once been present in the rotation will remain in it, but the mode of cultivation will be varied. You therefore quite consistently hope to meet your friends and acquaintances in a better world, but you do not share the fear of the crowd that they will be altered so that you cannot recognize them; your fear is rather lest they be wholly unaltered. It is remarkable how much significance even the most insignificant person can gain from a rational mode of cultivation. (*E/O I*, p. 291–292)

At first glance it might not appear as if this aesthetic account of friendship applies to the K man. After all *Seinfeld* is a show about nothing, but at least it is a show about nothing as it happens to four friends. I would suggest that despite the importance of friendship to *Seinfeld*, Kramer is remarkably non-committal in his friendships. Kramer could easily survive without George, Jerry, and Elaine. George and Elaine both need Jerry, and to some extent he needs them as well, but Kramer does not need

---

[7] For a different point of view on the necessity of friendship among the characters see Jennifer McMahon's "Seinfeld, Subjectivity, and Sartre," in this volume.

any of the other three and they do not need him.[7] More so than any of the other primary characters Kramer has cultivated other friendships/acquaintance relationships. He has many friends who do not intermingle with the main crew, most notably Bob Sacamano and Lomez. Jerry asks Kramer once why he never sees these other friends, "I'm beginning to think they don't exist." Kramer replies to Jerry, "They want to know why they never see you" ("The Frogger"). Kramer, of course, is also the only primary character to be friendly with the despicable yet merry Newman. In addition, Kramer at various times befriends visiting Japanese businessmen, the diminutive Mickey, a video-taping movie pirate, his caddy, a murderous former athlete, a soup Nazi, a group of smokers, Frank Costanza, Morty Seinfeld, and others. Further, at times Kramer packs his bags and seem-ingly leaves for good, once for a trip to Hollywood and once for his retirement in Del Boca Vista, Florida.

Each of the primary characters is selfish and in some ways incapable of a deep and meaningful friendship, but Kramer is perhaps the worst in this regard. How does Kramer treat the people who seem to be his closest friends? Most often, it seems he uses them as means to an end. Kramer became beloved by audiences for the wacky entrances he would make into Jerry's apartment, followed by the obligatory trip to Jerry's refrigerator. He freely helps himself to Jerry's food, and has no qualms about complaining when a desired item is missing or something is not up to snuff. He constantly borrows items, such as a Walkman, from Jerry and either does not return them or returns them bro-ken, claiming that was the condition in which he borrowed them. He routinely borrows Jerry's car and returns it on empty ("The Dealership"). Very childish, very aesthetic. When Elaine is away on vacation for over a month he does not even notice, insisting that he saw her just the other day ('The Butter Shave"). Certainly the other three primary characters are sources of amusement and camaraderie for Kramer, but he gets none too attached. He often spends time with his other "friends" when the regular fields need to lay fallow for a while. He chases some aesthetic project with others, whether returning bottles to Michigan with Newman or pursuing an acting career with Mickey. Eventually he will return to the other three, and hope-fully he will be able to discover something new and interesting about them to keep boredom and despair at bay.

When it comes down to it, all commitments including marriage, work, and friendship are to be avoided. Kramer, as the good aesthete, must remain free to act on his whims; he must be free to be arbitrary in his decisions. As A says, "One should always have an eye open for the accidental, always be *expeditus*, if anything should offer" (*E/O I,* p. 296). Clearly this is the position in which Kramer has strategically placed himself. He will amuse himself with the slightest variation in his environment at a moment's notice. As the A man puts it, and as the K man would surely agree,

> The whole secret lies in arbitrariness. People usually think it easy to be arbitrary, but it requires much study to succeed in being arbitrary so as not to lose oneself in it, but so as to derive satisfaction from it. (*E/O I,* p. 295)

Kramer the "Seducer"

In *Either/Or* vol. I Kierkegaard presents us with the fictional "Diary of the Seducer." The seducer, Johannes, is a perfect aesthete seeking to win the heart of a young girl, Cordelia, simply for the sport of it. Let us review briefly this "Diary of the Seducer" and note the parallels to Kramer's aestheticism in matters of love.

Bearing witness to the aestheticism of Johannes the seducer, the presenter of the diary tells us the following:

> His life had been an attempt to realize the task of living poetically. With a keenly developed interest in life, he had known how to find it, and after finding it, he constantly reproduced the experience more or less poetically. (*E/O I,* p. 300)

> He lived far too intellectually to be a seducer in the common understanding of the word. (*E/O I,* p. 303)

While, to the extent that he is an aesthete, Kramer lives poetically, remembering and forgetting what he will and crafting his life like an art work in progress, few, if any, would accuse him of living intellectually. Still, like Johannes, it may be fair to say of him that he is not a seducer in the ordinary understanding of the word.

Johannes's aim and strategy are more playful than malicious, at least in their intent if not in their results. He is neither a gross misogynist nor a man in need of mere ego gratification. Rather, he seeks to construct an artful scenario, full of tension and expectation, a dramatic poem telling the story of a love not to be. The presenter of the diary describes the seducer's mode of operation in the following way:

> By the aid of his intellectual endowments he had known how to tempt a young girl and attract her to himself, without really caring to possess her. I can imagine that he knew how to excite a girl to the highest pitch, so that he was certain she was ready to sacrifice everything. When the affair reached this point, he broke it off without himself having made the slightest advances and without having let fall a single word of love, let alone a declaration, a promise. (*E/O I*, pp. 302–303)

The seducer seeks to stimulate his own interest, and to cater to his need for change in his romantic pursuits, as in all other pursuits. Yet in the romantic scenario he is not completely selfish in his need for "the interesting," but seeks to involve the object of his desire in the interesting as well. To be sure, this is part of his strategy but it would also be less than fitting if the desired girl did not find the pursuit adventuresome and interesting. As Johannes the seducer puts it,

> [T]he strategic principle, the law governing every move in this campaign, is always to work her into an interesting situation. The interesting is the field on which this battle must be waged; the potentialities of the interesting must be exhausted. Unless I am mistaken, her whole nature is designed for this, so that what I require is exactly what she gives, indeed, what she herself requires. (*E/O I*, p. 341)

Johannes is clear about his aestheticism and the role that the erotic plays in it. "Under the heaven of the aesthetic, everything is light, beautiful, transitory; when the ethical comes along, then everything becomes harsh, angular, infinitely boring" (*E/O I*, p. 363). The seducer arranges things so that any engagement will be broken off by the woman; indeed anything he wants the woman does; anything he desires the woman gives of her own free will. He is a composer conducting his own symphony. "I have reached the point where I desire nothing which is not, in the strictest sense, freely given. Let common seducers use such methods" (*E/O I*, p. 363). The seducer is the artist of erotic love; it is the clay which he molds to suit his desire, or at least so he believes.

> I am an aesthete, an eroticist, one who has understood the nature and meaning of love, who believes in love who knows it from the ground up, and only makes the private reservation that no love affair should last more than six months at the most, and that every erotic relationship should cease as soon as one has had the ultimate enjoyment. I know all this, I know, too, that the highest conceivable enjoyment lies in being loved; to be loved is higher than anything else in the world. To poetize oneself into a young girl is an art, to poetize oneself out of her is a masterpiece. (*E/O I*, p. 363–64)

Kramer too is an aesthetic eroticist. It is true that he does not display the kind of poetic artfulness that Johannes does, but he nonetheless fits the bill. As we noticed in discussing the crop rotation, Kramer makes not even the slightest gesture towards marriage,[8] nor does he ever have a meaningful relationship with a woman. Yet Kramer is not left wanting for romantic encounters. Indeed, he most often gets involved with women who are seemingly unattainable or unavailable. Consider some of Kramer's love interests: the lesbian lover of George's ex-girlfriend Susan, a nun/novice in the Latvian Orthodox Church, the "quite fetching" Pam (with the help of Newman à la Cyrano de Bergerac), a "low talker," Gail (whom he snubbed at first for not going further with Jerry), and the woman who walked naked in front of her window, thus quickly bringing an end to "the contest." How does he do it? As Kramer tells us, he has a power called the "Kavorca," Latvian for "lure of the animal." Witness his own awe at this strange gift, "Oh, this power! Look what I'm doing! I'm dangerous, Jerry! I'm very dangerous" ("The Conversion")!

The story lines do not ordinarily tell us how Kramer's seduction stories end, however. We never actually see how his rela-

---

[8] Though at one point Elaine and he agree to get married in fifty years if nothing else pans out.

tionships come to an end, and in one case we are even left wondering: Has he really *slipped one past the goalie?* We can be sure,
however, that he does usually experience the "ultimate enjoyment." It also seems a pretty safe bet that he shows some side
of himself to his love interests which makes them all too glad to
go away of their own accord. With the revolving door of
women, Kramer the aesthete manages to keep his life interesting, free from boredom and despair. If asked how he does it,
our aesthetic eroticist would simply reply, "I'm Kramer."

Kramer and the Ethical

Kierkegaard presents the standpoint of the ethical stage in
Either/Or vol. II.[9] In this work, again edited by the pseudonymous Victor Eremita, Judge William speaks on behalf of the ethical life, in some cases writing letters to the aesthete A. As we
have seen, Kramer is clearly mired in the aesthetic stage, with
little hope, it would seem, of moving beyond it. Yet we can
profit from considering what he might be like if he did indeed
move into the ethical sphere of existence. Let us first describe
the ethical stage in greater detail and then depict Kramer as
within in it. There is in fact one episode, "The Bizarro Jerry," in
which Kramer flirts with the ethical, and we shall use this as our
guide.

The aesthetic stage ends, as it began, in despair. In the ethical stage, then, one escapes from the despair that was underlying the constant change ("rotation") of the aesthetic stage. The
aesthete is without commitment; he never chooses with firm
resolve and so is never truly tied to any person, place, or thing.
By contrast, the ethical stage is marked by commitment; one
commits oneself to the universal, to what society values. The
aesthete, as we noted, is amoral, not taking moral norms seriously. By contrast, the ethical person feels firmly bound to duty
and obligation. He takes quite seriously moral commands of the
form "Honor thy father and thy mother" and "Thou shalt not
bear false witness against thy neighbor." These commands, and

---

[9] Søren Kierkegaard, *Either/Or* volume II. Trans. Howard V. Hong and Edna
H. Hong (Princeton: Princeton University Press, 1987). Further references
to this book are indicated in parentheses by *E/O II* accompanied by page
numbers.

others of similar form, are seen as universal, as binding on everyone at all times. The aesthete might obey such commands, but she would do so only when it suited her needs or satisfied her desires. She would follow them simply as a means to an end. Think, for example, of Kramer's boycott of Kenny Rogers Roasters. His motivation is not principled but practical; the glare from the store's neon sign is disturbing him as he tries to sleep. When Jerry switches apartments with him, Kramer yields to Newman's temptation and begins to feast on the tasty bird. By contrast, the ethical person sees universal commands and principled stands as part of the very purpose of life; following such commands is an end in itself.

Whereas one may be inclined to think of the adolescent as the paradigm of aesthetic existence, one may be inclined to think of the family man or woman as the paradigm of ethical existence. It is no coincidence that Kierkegaard chooses William, a family man and judge, to be the spokesperson for the ethical life. Kierkegaard himself lived aesthetically through a good number of his student years but eventually could hide from the despair no longer and took up the ethical mode of existence. He courted Regine Olsen, the love of his life, and completed his studies in preparation for the ministry. He embraced the values of society and had what everyone desired, a beautiful woman who loved him and a promising career on the horizon. This was not to last, though, as we shall discuss in the context of our examination of the religious stage. In moving into the ethical stage, Kierkegaard found refuge from his despair, but it was at the cost of his individuality. This is typical.

The person in the ethical stage, despite perhaps having given up on individuality, sees himself as more free than the person who is in the aesthetic stage. This is ironic in that the aesthete perceives himself as utterly free, doing whatever he wants whenever he wants. In the eyes of the ethical person this is not freedom at all. Rather, it is being controlled by one's impulses, like a ship being tossed on the ocean. It is only when one follows the universal, the moral rules which apply to all people in all cases, that one is truly free. Judge William puts the matter in the following way:

> For me, the moment of choosing is very earnest, not so much because of the rigorous thinking through of what appears sepa-

rated in the choice, not because of the multiplicity of thoughts linked to each particular element, but because there is danger involved, that in the very next moment a choice may not be at my disposal . . . (*E/O II,* p. 164)

Your choice is an esthetic choice, but an esthetic choice is no choice. On the whole, to choose is an intrinsic and stringent term for the ethical. (*E/O II,* p. 166)

Now, if you are to understand me properly, I may very well say that what is important in choosing is not so much to choose the right thing as the energy, the earnestness, and the pathos with which one chooses. (*E/O II,* p. 167)

[T]he esthetic in a person is that by which he spontaneously and immediately is what he is; the ethical is that by which he becomes what he becomes. (*E/O II,* p. 178)

Judge William, as spokesperson for the ethical, makes clear that the aesthete never really chooses, in that what appear to be choices are mere acts of whim lacking in commitment. The aesthetic choice is no choice. By contrast, the ethical choice is truly a choice in the best sense of the word. It is made with serious nature, mindful of the consequences, and in belief that the same choice should be made by all people under the same circumstances. There is no guarantee that we are right in our beliefs regarding what is or should be universal, but we must choose those beliefs with full commitment. It is through making such choices that we become who we are. There is a steady course of development in becoming what one becomes in the ethical. By contrast, the aesthete is, to use Judge William's words, what he is immediately and spontaneously.

What would it take for Kramer to move from the aesthetic to the ethical? He would have to become tired of his ceaseless "rotation" of harebrained schemes and diversions. Once these diversions could no longer keep his underlying despair at bay, he might then be ready for the ethical stage. Certainly, as we leave Kramer at the conclusion of the series he is still deeply entrenched in the aesthetic stage. He, along with the other three primary characters, has been sentenced to a year in jail, for violating a Good Samaritan law by failing to come to the aid of a car-jacking victim. He and the others make no choice to help or not help but simply enjoy the spectacle—very aesthetic of them.[10] The sentence of one year in jail does nothing to awaken Kramer (or the others it seems). He sees it as *not such a bad thing,* three meals a day, *yada yada yada.*

There is one episode, however, in which Kramer flirts with the ethical. This, as mentioned above, is "The Bizarro Jerry." In this episode Kramer ventures into the business world. After using the men's room at Brandt Leland, Kramer is pulled into a meeting, and for a short time works at the company, though not technically an employee. He remarks to Jerry, who becomes much like his wife in this episode, that this is just what he needed, "structure." "I don't know if you've noticed it lately Jerry, but I've been drifting." "Now that you mentioned it . . ." Jerry replies. Kramer describes his work as "TCB, taking care of business." He falls in love with the corporate world, taking the "morning train," working long hours, wearing a suit, going to meetings. All of these are indicative of the values of the person in the ethical stage. The structure, rules, and duty are taken quite seriously. Despair is gone, but individuality is lost. After a very brief tenure Kramer is fired from Brandt Leland, though as he explains, "I don't even work here." Even if Kramer had not been fired it is unlikely that he would have stuck with the job. It would most likely have been just another aesthetic adventure. But, then again, who knows?

Kramer and the Religious

Kierkegaard gives his clearest depiction of the religious stage in *Fear and Trembling,*[11] presented by the pseudonymous Johannes de Silentio. Because of its paradoxical nature, the religious stage is perhaps the most difficult to understand. Johannes himself does not claim to fully understand it but rather to have a view to it through the biblical account of Abraham and Isaac (Genesis 22: 1–19). Moving to the religious stage is no easy mat-

---

[10] For further discussion of this see the final essay in this volume, "The Final Episode: Is Doing Nothering Something?"

[11] Søren Kierkegaard, *Fear and Trembling/Repetition.* Trans. Howard V. Hong and Edna H. Hong (Princeton: Princeton University Press, 1983). Further references to this book are indicated in parentheses by *FT* accompanied by page numbers.

ter; it involves a leap, a "leap of faith." In the religious stage the
individual paradoxically becomes higher than the universal.
"Faith is namely this paradox that the single individual is higher
than the universal" (*FT,* p. 55). The universal commands of society, followed so strictly in the ethical stage, are eclipsed by the
divine command. For this reason, the story of Abraham and
Isaac is the perfect depiction of the religious stage. Abraham and
his wife Sarah have reached old age without having a son.
Miraculously, the aged Sarah does conceive and give birth to a
son, Isaac. God has smiled upon them, but now God asks for
the son back, so to speak. Abraham is commanded to sacrifice
Isaac to the Lord. Although he loves his son and wants very
much for him to carry on the family legacy, Abraham is willing
to sacrifice Isaac. Beyond that, Abraham is willing to bypass the
ethical commandment against murder. The universal law
declares: "Thou shalt not kill." In this case, Abraham is willing
to suspend the ethical, what Kierkegaard calls a "teleological
suspension of the ethical," in favor of his duty to God. As we all
know, in the end, God spares the life of Isaac, providing a ram
for the sacrifice. Because he was willing to give up what he
cherished most, Abraham was rewarded. His son and heir, Isaac,
would survive; Isaac would beget Jacob, *yada yada yada.* And
so began the Kingdom of Israel.

Kierkegaard saw the events of his own life as paralleling the
story of Abraham and Isaac. Having settled into a comfortable
life with the prospects of a beautiful wife and rewarding job (his
ethical stage), Kierkegaard decided to sacrifice it all. He broke
his engagement with Regine, believing that God had commanded him to devote himself to his writing in a way that a
married man never could. Nearly to the end Kierkegaard held
out hope that God would somehow reunite him with Regine,
just as he had given Isaac back to Abraham, but Kierkegaard
was not so fortunate as was Abraham.

We should note both the absurdity and the difficulty involved
in making the leap of faith into the religious stage. Truth, for
Kierkegaard, is a subjective matter. In matters of faith, one
should not seek proof or justification, but rather one must
believe out of passion. The early Church Father Tertullian said,
"I believe because it is absurd." Kierkegaard echoes that sentiment, arguing that live and passionate belief embraces the
absurd. Kierkegaard calls a figure such as Abraham, who has

made the leap of faith to the religious stage, a knight of faith. In calling him a knight, there is an implicit reference to the bravery required to make the leap. It is not easy, but is made in "fear and trembling." There is no faith without doubt, after all. "The knight of faith realizes . . . he can be saved only by the absurd, and this he grasps by faith" (*FT,* p. 47).

It is the rare individual who makes the leap of faith to the religious stage. Some of us remain in the aesthetic stage our entire lives, while others move to the ethical stage and remain there. To be clear, religious belief alone is not sufficient for being in the religious stage. The Sunday churchgoer is by no means necessarily in the religious stage. The religious stage requires a level of faith that is rarely seen, a faith that one knows one's duty to God, accompanied by the commitment to carry out that duty at all costs and despite all appearances. This is a truly profound state in which to dwell.

So, what about Kramer? As we leave him at the end of the series he is not even in the ethical stage. Although one does not necessarily pass through all three stages in life, one must take them in order. Let us imagine for a moment what would happen if Kramer did move to the ethical stage. Had he escaped despair and taken up the ethical life, working for Brandt Leland, getting married and having children, and, God forbid, even moving out of Manhattan to Connecticut, would Kramer be satisfied? I suggest that he would not. While many of us can spend our lives lost in the workaday world, I suggest that Kramer would soon tire of this. Kramer, like Kierkegaard himself, is first and foremost an individual, and the loss of individuality in the ethical stage would not sit well with him. He would need something higher and better. In the most genuine sense, individuality is achieved in the religious stage when one becomes aware of one's unique duty to the divine. I can imagine Kramer throwing it all away like Paul Gaugin. Kramer, feeling the call to Jerusalem, Mecca, or some mountaintop in Tibet, might indeed go. One of the many rumored endings for the series was along these very lines: Kramer finds God.[12] As strange as that sounds, it might be plausible. After all, if the divinity has a unique plan in mind for anyone, it must be Kramer!

---

[12] See Jason Alexander's August 1997 *Playboy* interview, "Alexander The Great," p. 158.

Conclusion

Strange bedfellows indeed, Kramer and Kierkegaard. Still, I hope this brief tour through Kierkegaard's "stages on life's way" guided by *Seinfeld*'s most beloved nutball has shed some light on each of them. And at the very least it was fun to consider, *not that there's anything wrong with that.*[13]

---

[13] I wish to thank Robert Guldner, Marc Marchese, and Vanessa DeMartino for very helpful comments on an earlier draft of this essay. I also wish to thank Heather McDonough and my other students who drew my attention to the connection between *Seinfeld* and Kierkegaard.

Act II

Seinfeld and the Philosophers

5
Making Something out of Nothing: *Seinfeld*, Sophistry, and the Tao

ERIC BRONSON

Every true *Seinfeld* fan knows the basic premise of the sitcom: it's a show about nothing, or so it has been said. People stand around, chitchatting, not doing *anything*. For nine years, Americans actually looked forward to spending thirty minutes a week watching and enjoying . . . nothing? Jerry Seinfeld isn't the first comedian to think there is something unmistakably funny in nothing. Over four hundred years ago, William Shakespeare, the most popular slapstick comedian in the Western world, wrote a whimsical play that was "Much Ado about Nothing." Apparently nothingness not only exists, it can also make people laugh.

Seinfeld and the Problem of a Show about Nothing

Before proceeding, we must pose the philosophical question, does it make sense to even talk about nothing? There is a well-known recurring *Seinfeld* story line in which George and Jerry hatch their idea for an NBC television show called *Jerry*.[1]

---

[1] The primary shows dealing with this story line are: "The Pitch/The Ticket," "The Wallet," "The Watch," "The Cheever Letters," "The Shoes," "The Pilot," and "The Finale."

(The character Jerry is, of course, spoofing real life Jerry and his show about nothing.)[2] In Monk's coffee shop (where else?), George explains to Jerry how the show will revolutionize television because it will be about absolutely nothing. Jerry cuts in, claiming that of course the show has to be about something, but George is adamant. He envisions people standing around an office water cooler and nothing happens. Nothing at all. Just like real life. Or is it?

Does "nothing" happen in real life? Unknowingly, George has hit on one of the world's most fundamental philosophical questions. Does nothingness exist in the world, and if it does then how can we know it? Philosophers, in both the East and the West, first articulated this question over two thousand years ago. Let's first examine the historical roots of the issue before judging whether George's vision for a show about nothingness is philosophically sound.

Parmenides, Plato, and Nothing

The year was around 450 B.C. and the famous philosopher Parmenides came to Athens to talk about nothing (sound familiar?). He claimed that in every philosophical discussion, a person could either talk about something that exists or something that does not exist. But, according to Parmenides, it is impossible to genuinely express a thought about something that does not exist. How do we know something does not exist? We are inclined to think that "a square circle does not exist," but for this statement to be true, we need to know what a square circle is. We must know our subject before we can test the truth of the statement. The statement is composed of the subject, "square circle," and the predicate, "does not exist." Before we agree or disagree, we need to know what a square circle is, but this is precisely the problem. We cannot know what a square circle is because it does not exist. Therefore, according to Parmenides, it is impossible to know, and foolish to say, anything about something that does not exist. We cannot say anything meaningful about nothing.

---

[2] For a discussion of the relationship between the character Jerry Seinfeld and the person Jerry Seinfeld see William Irwin's "Jerry and Socrates: The Examined Life?" in this volume.

Let's take another example. George Costanza might say that Mr. Art Vandelay is not a real person (at least until he meets the judge by that name in the final episode). We who have seen *Seinfeld*, and know that Vandelay is simply a name that George uses to get out of difficult situations, might be inclined to agree. However, according to Parmenides, we are all misguided. We are trying to say something factual about a person who does not exist. By talking about Vandelay we are saying something about nothing and, over 2,000 years ago, this was not particularly funny!

Socrates took Parmenides' thoughts on nothing pretty seriously. So did his disciple Plato, who later wrote a dialogue on Socrates's points of disagreement with Parmenides. That dialogue, entitled the *Sophist*, is Plato's defense of nothing. In it he not only argues that nothingness is an existing force in the world, but also insists that there is an element of nothing in everything we say and know. In other words, every show on television is partially about something and partially about nothing.

Sophists in ancient Greece were traveling wise men who went from town to town teaching the art of argumentation. For a small fee, they would provide convincing arguments on any subject their clients wished. They could be especially useful in courts of law where persuading the jury was often far more important to a defendant's case than uncovering the truth. Their reliance on persuasion naturally set them at odds with the new philosophers of Athens who believed in the pursuit of truth above all else. Sophists oftentimes resorted to reasoning that was based not on what actually existed but on what did not exist. In other words, they too tried to make something out of nothing!

In Plato's dialogue the *Sophist*, a "Stranger" to Athens attempts to understand exactly what kind of person the Sophist is. To reach this insight he engages Plato's friend and colleague, Theaetetus, in a heated debate on the issue. It is difficult to adequately define the Sophist since he seems to be a number of people rolled up in one (in Greece, the forked tongue was a distinctly male characteristic). Still, the two philosophers set out to hunt down the Sophist (delineate who exactly he is) using their weapon of choice, dialectic reasoning. Theaetetus and the Stranger pledge to "follow hard upon [the Sophist], constantly dividing the part that gives him shelter, until he is caught."[3] At first glance, the hunt for the Sophist does not seem too imposing. We can simply say that a Sophist is a fast talker, a shyster, and a quack. Or, to put it more elegantly, "the Sophist possesses a sort of reputed and apparent knowledge on all subjects, but not the reality."[4] But there is a problem with this approach. The Sophist makes many untrue claims and therefore resides in a world that does not exist. Parmenides had argued that it is impossible to say anything intelligible about something that does not exist, and so it seems as if the Sophist has surrounded himself with nothing. He has secured himself the ideal hiding place: a haunt nobody can reach, in a realm of which no human mind can conceive.

Now we can see why George meets such initial resistance from the top brass at NBC. What would a show about nothing look like? By even talking about the show, George appears foolish since anything he says about the plot can only be analyzed if it applies to *something* that really exists. For George's show to be accepted by philosophic minds he would need to first convince the executives that nothing is something that really exists. An argument along Platonic lines might have made him a wealthy man. Instead, George tries to ask an executive out on a date and ends up at the dry cleaners after she vomits on his shirt.

Plato's Stranger knows that in order to reach the Sophist, who is shrouded in things that do not exist, he needs to articulate something substantial about nothing, the very pursuit that Parmenides claimed to be futile. "We shall find it necessary in self-defense to put to the question that pronouncement of father Parmenides, and establish by main force that what is not, in some respect has being, and conversely that what is, in a way is not."[5] In other words, if the Stranger can prove that nothing is also something, then he can say something meaningful about it, thus pinning down the identity of the slippery Sophist.

---

[3] *Sophist,* translated by F. M. Cornford, 235c, in Edith Hamilton and Huntington Cairns eds., *Collected Dialogues of Plato* (Princeton: Princeton University Press, 1961).
[4] Ibid., 233c.
[5] Ibid., 241d.

Plato's Stranger insists that there has to be something to nothing. To support his claim, he uses the example of something that is "not-beautiful." When we claim something is not beautiful the subject still *is* something; it *is* something that is not beautiful. Take, for example, Jerry's puffy shirt that he unwittingly agrees to wear on the *Today Show* ("The Puffy Shirt"). Surely this is not a beautiful shirt. However, even its most ardent critics must agree that the shirt is something; it is something *other* than beautiful. Everything that exists seems to have this quality of otherness. Elaine is a *Seinfeld* character who is *other* than shy. Kramer's coordination is something that is *other* than graceful. And, yes, George's proposed show could be about people doing nothing, if we think of them as doing something *other* than what is interesting or useful. In fact, this is usually the case with *Seinfeld* and it is the case with the episodes of *Jerry*, which George claims will be about nothing. Consider the famous episode "The Parking Garage." In this episode the gang is stuck doing nothing, or at least something other than what is interesting or useful. They look in vain for the car they parked somewhere (who knows where?) in a mall parking garage. In this episode Jerry actually reflects on doing nothing, or at least not doing what he imagines other people do.

JERRY: Why do I always have this feeling that everybody's doing something better than me on Saturday afternoons?

ELAINE: This is what people do.

JERRY: No they don't. They're out on some big picnic. They're cooking burgers, making out on blankets. They're not in some mall in Jersey watching their friends try to find the world's cheapest air conditioner. ("The Parking Garage")

In the *Sophist*, the Stranger concludes that nothingness does indeed contain an element of something. It contains something of otherness. And, according to this line of reasoning, something also contains an element of nothing. After all, even something beautiful is still something *other* than ugly. Art Vandelay is someone; he is someone other than a real person. *Seinfeld* and *Jerry* are about something, something other than what is normally considered interesting or useful. There is something in nothing and nothing in something, even though Parmenides called this blurry mixing a sure sign of "backward thinking."[6] If Plato is right to resurrect this backward thinking then even the Sophist's statements are something since they are something *other* than the truth. The light of reason can again reveal the Sophist's shadowy hideout and the philosophical hunters can circle their prey, learning something about nothing along the way.

Before we leave the West behind, however, let's observe one other feature of Plato's nothingness, its power. We have observed how the Platonic nothing is something, it is real and it has being. But what does it mean for something to be real? Plato has the Stranger answer:

> I suggest that anything has real being that is so constituted as to possess any sort of power, either to affect anything else or to be affected, in however small a degree, by the most insignificant agent, though it be only once. I am proposing as a mark to distinguish real things that *they are nothing but power.*[7]

Since nothingness has real being, it must have real power. For Plato, nothingness is a power in the world that pervades all existing and non-existing things. Whether this nothingness has the power to make us laugh is another question altogether, and one that, regrettably, Plato did not answer but has left for us.

The Tao of *Seinfeld*

At about the same time Plato was hunting for the Sophist in his nothing disguise, across the globe in Asia there was a similar interest in *nothing* in particular. The Buddha (560–480 B.C.) in India and Lao Tzu (around 575 B.C.) in China believed that peace and happiness were the earthly rewards for properly understanding nothing. In the interest of brevity, let's restrict ourselves to examining only the latter. Lao Tzu's *Tao Te Ching,* or *The Way of Life,* continues to hold a pre-eminent place in

---

[6] An excellent translation and analysis of Parmenides's Hexameter Poem can be found in *The Pre-Socratic Philosophers,* edited by Kirk, Raven, and Schofield, (Cambridge: Cambridge University Press, 1983), pp. 239–262.
[7] *Sophist,* 247e (italics mine).

Eastern philosophy; even the rapid spread of Buddhism into Japan and China succeeded only as far as it could be adapted to basic Taoist precepts.

Lao Tzu frequently talked of something and nothing and, unlike Parmenides, he was not afraid of backward thinking. What is the Tao? This is not an easy question, and, in fact, it is *the* question that Lao Tzu's entire book of poems attempts to answer. The first thing that is said of the Tao is that nothing can be said of it. "Tao called Tao is not Tao."[8] In other words, the Tao is not something and therefore it can not be described as such. All we can accurately say of it is that it is nameless and yet all of life's secrets reside in this mystical Tao.

Jerry and George clearly do not know Chinese philosophy, but they do know Chinese food. In fact one of George's plot ideas for *Jerry*, his show about nothing, is an episode in which people in a Chinese restaurant stand in line for a table. This, of course, was already the basis for an earlier *Seinfeld* episode, "The Chinese Restaurant." The entire episode featured Jerry, George, and Elaine waiting for a table until the show ends with them leaving the restaurant hungry and irritable. It seems as though nothing happens in the entire show; they don't even get their Chinese dinner.[9] George, as we know, claims this is true to life since nothing ever happens. Lao Tzu disagrees.

As we have noted, nothingness is at the root of the nameless Tao. In contrast to George's show about nothing, however, Taoists believe that nothing does make something happen. In fact, Taoist nothingness is said to have created everything in the world.[10]

---

[8] *Tao Te Ching,* translated by Stephen Addiss and Stanley Lombardo, (Indianapolis: Hackett, 1993), ch. 1.

[9] Other *Seinfeld* episodes about *nothing* in particular include: "The Parking Garage," "The Subway," "The Movie," "The Dinner Party," and to a lesser extent "The Puerto Rican Day."

[10] The idea of the world being created from nothingness is not entirely unfamiliar to the West. Medieval religious mystics had highly sophisticated theories about how the Judeo-Christian God created the world *ex-nihilo* (from nothing). The Jewish Kabbalah even hints that God himself may have been born from nothing.

> Tao engenders One,
> One engenders Two,
> Two engenders Three,
> Three engenders the ten thousand things.[11]

The Tao that is nameless, the Tao that is not something, is so powerful that it creates ten thousand things. And to think George can't even get a table at a Chinese restaurant.

The *Tao Te Ching* encourages people to live their lives according to the Tao in order to live happily and tranquilly. But how is this possible? First of all, we need to understand the Taoist conception of *wu wei*, or non-action. The idea is simple but nevertheless maddening to the Western reader who has been inculcated to "Just do it." The Tao commands us not to do it, or more accurately, to do nothing.

> Act and you ruin it.
> Grasp and you lose it.
> Therefore the Sage
> Does not act *(Wu wei)*
> And so does not ruin
> Does not grasp
> And so does not lose.[12]

At first glance, *wu wei* surely seems like a losing attitude. It's not often one hears a college professor telling her class to go home and do nothing. And yet, this is precisely what the Tao demands.

> Pursue knowledge, gain daily.
> Pursue Tao, lose daily.
> Lose and again lose,
> Arrive at non-doing.
>
> Non-doing *(Wu wei)*—and nothing not done.[13]

Gaining knowledge daily is seen as harmful if the knowledge gained is only wordplay. Words are only useful if they can help point the way to the inexpressible and unnamed Tao.

---

[11] *Tao Te Ching,* ch. 42.
[12] Ibid., ch. 64.
[13] Ibid., ch 48.

When one does nothing in the right way, nothing is left undone. Taoists believe that doing nothing is in fact doing something and such a paradox is expressed by the phrase *wei wu wei,* or action by non-action. The idea behind *wei wu wei* is that one can become strong through weakness, one conquers by doing nothing. In the *Tao Te Ching,* stiffness and strength are characteristics of death. The living human organism is soft and weak, hardening only after rigor mortis has set in.

The strong and great sink down.
The soft and weak rise up.[14]

In Christian theology, it is said that the meek shall inherit the earth someday. In Taoist philosophy, the meek, who do nothing, inherit the earth in *this* lifetime.

How then does weakness conquer? There is a story in Zen Buddhist lore that exhibits quite succinctly the Taoist action by non-action. Once upon a time, there was a sword that was highly regarded by samurai warriors because of its blade, which could kill instantly. When placed in a river, the sword immediately severed all of the leaves that crossed its path. As the story goes, another swordsmith claimed to have an even stronger sword, though anyone could see the blade was not as sharp as the first sword. However, when this second sword was placed in the river, a funny thing happened. No leaf was severed because none dared to cross its path.[15] This second sword did nothing and yet it changed the natural course of leaves flowing down a river. By doing nothing, everything moved out of its way.

But we do not need to dip into ancient Eastern lore to test the practicality of action by non-action. We have seen it conquer in the United States in this century. In the 1950s and 1960s Martin Luther King Jr. and his non-violent army showed the world how doing nothing inevitably brings down the high and mighty. In Alabama, white officers of the law armed themselves with rifles, hand guns, knives, clubs, dogs, and even hoses. The black protesters carried nothing, and more importantly, they did nothing. First, they boycotted the transportation system, bring-

[14] Ibid., ch. 76.
[15] Daisetz Suzuki relates this story in *Zen and Japanese Culture* (Princeton: Princeton University Press, 1993), p. 92.

ing the local economy to its knees, by doing *nothing*! After the boycotts, they began peaceful marches. Of course, as we know, the marches did not always end so peacefully. In the beginning, the rifles, guns, knives, clubs, dogs, and hoses were winning the fight. However, as the Tao states, "The softest thing in the world rides roughshod over the strongest."[16] This proved to be prophetic as popular sympathy and support slowly mounted on the side of the protesters. The strong were laid low, and the weak became strong.

Taoist nothingness, then, is not a handbook for cowards. It takes tremendous mental discipline, fortitude, and courage to do nothing. *Wei wu wei* is one of the world's oldest recipes for conquering the enemy. Action by non-action is the inner rhythm of the Tao. As soldiers of the Tao, human beings must learn the rigorous discipline of doing something by doing nothing. If successful, the *Tao Te Ching* promises us all the ten thousand things of the world. And that is nothing to laugh at.

Was it a Show about Nothing?

Now let's return to poor George Costanza and his proposed show about nothing. The NBC executives were skeptical to the end, finally accepting the proposal after Jerry and George agreed to make something happen. But George never wanted something to happen, therefore pitting himself against a two thousand-year history of philosophy in the East and West. Plato long ago claimed that there is always something in nothing and vice versa. And, as any Taoist will tell you, non-action, properly understood, always makes something happen. Therefore, if nothing ever happened in George's show, such a concept would be more revolutionary than even he himself imagined.

The real-life Seinfeld believes the joke is on us since his show about nothing lasted nine years. Did something come from nothing or did only nothing happen? If viewers really did not see anything happen then we might want to rethink our conceptions of nothingness since Plato and Lao Tzu insist there is something to nothing. Then again, maybe nothing in *Seinfeld* is funny. Now that would be something.[17]

---

[16] *Tao Te Ching,* ch. 43.
[17] Thanks to Brian and Paul Horan for their expertise and for unrestricted use of their video library.

6
Plato or Nietzsche?: Time, Essence, and Eternal Recurrence in *Seinfeld*

MARK T. CONARD

"*End and goal.* Not every end is a goal. The end of a melody is not its goal; but nonetheless, if the melody had not reached its end it would not have reached its goal either. A parable."

—Nietzsche[1]

"Know why fish are so thin? They only eat fish."

—Jerry Seinfeld[2]

Time as a Problem

Time is an essential part of comedy, of humor. As comedians say, "timing is everything." The Nietzsche passage above talks about music, about a melody line: the purpose of the line of music is not to get to the end, but if it hasn't gotten to the end it hasn't served its purpose. We can extrapolate this to humor.

---

[1] Friedrich Nietzsche, *Human, All too Human,* "The Wanderer and his Shadow," p. 204.
[2] Jerry Seinfeld, episode 44, "The Watch."

The purpose of a joke, a quip, a witticism, or a pun is not to get to the end, the punch line, but if the joke hasn't reached the punch line, it won't have reached its goal.

What is the purpose of a joke? To get a laugh, of course. So the point isn't just to get to the punch line, to get it out there. The point is to produce a certain effect. And to produce that effect, timing is necessary. The joke has to be set up, prepared, and an expectation has to be established in the listener. If we say, "Fish only eat fish, that's why they're so thin," it's not funny. We've gotten the punch line out, but we've blown the joke.

Humor is something that relies on and makes use of language much of the time. But it's not simple communication, of course. If I want to communicate some information, very often the order in which I communicate it will not have any effect on what is communicated, except in cases where slight confusion is created. But that is easily remedied. If I say, "Mary is bright, and she's pretty," I am saying the same thing as "Mary is pretty, and she's bright." If I have omitted saying who Mary is, which Mary I am referring to, I can always go back and tack on that information. "I mean Mary Stevens." "Oh, that Mary!" you reply. The situation has been fixed; the confusion evaporates.

Try fixing a joke after you've already told it poorly. It's easier to sum up Nietzsche's philosophy in 25 words or less.

There are many factors involved in telling a joke well, of course. The way the voice is inflected can be important; the material itself has to be good; funny shoes don't hurt. But the key is the order in which the lines are said and the pauses that are thrown in to build the expectation. The key is timing. Time is a problem for comedians.

But time is a human problem or concern in a general sense. This makes it a philosophical issue. We must first consider finitude. Human beings are finite creatures. We only have so much time. It is our finitude, our limited time, which gives structure to our lives, and sense and meaning to our projects. If we lived forever, if we literally had all the time in the world, there would be much less, if any, sense and meaning to the things we do with our lives. If I were immortal, what difference would it make if I chose to do this as opposed to that, for next year or a hundred centuries from now I could do that too. Nothing lost, nothing gained by the choices I make. Since we are mortal, because we only have so much time, our choices become significant, meaningful. "I have wasted my time," I can say with regret.

Some philosophers identify human beings most closely with consciousness. I am my consciousness, my subjectivity. But consciousness is essentially temporal. The philosopher Immanuel Kant (1724–1804) argued that space is the form of outer sense, meaning that I perceive things in the world around me in space. That is clear enough. The desk is directly in front of me, the phone two feet to my left, the bed four feet behind me, and my hometown is five hundred fifty miles away. But time is the form of inner sense. My thoughts—the inner monologue that is my awareness of myself—are not in space. Ideas don't have spatial dimension, but they are in time. The inner monologue is the flow of my thoughts; and flowing means anticipating the future, existing in the present, and disappearing into the past.

I spoke of past, present, and future. Existentialist philosophers, among others, make sharp distinctions between human reality and the reality of things or objects. Ordinary things or objects are fixed in their existences in the here and now. The desk is what it is *now*, and it's the same as it was then, and the same as it will ever be as long as it is in existence. Everything is here now for the desk to be what it is. No mystery, nothing lacking. It is complete, now, in the present.

I wouldn't say the same of myself. In no way at all is everything that's here and now all there is to me. My past is essential to who and what I am. And I'm continually dragging it along behind me. My past makes sense of my present. The thoughts I'm having, the actions I'm performing, and the plans I'm making only make sense, given what and who I was two minutes ago, five days ago, fifteen years ago. Further, my present only makes sense in terms of a projected future. I leave the house with the intention of going to the university. I enter the restaurant expecting to meet my friend and have lunch. Without the anticipation of the future, the intentions, and the expectations, my present has no meaning. For human beings, the present almost disappears with the wake of the past trailing along behind it and with the future bearing down upon it. Time is a philosophical issue, a philosophical problem.

Now, given the importance of temporality to human existence, philosophers and scientists have offered a number of different ways of understanding time, different ways of trying to figure out exactly what time is. Isaac Newton, for example, held the notion of absolute time (as well as absolute space). This is probably the way we normally think about time, if we reflect on it. Newton's idea is that the movement of hands on a clock, and other such processes, measure what's called relative time. This time is relative to the never-ending flow of the real time of the world. The latter, then, is the absolute time and cannot itself be measured, since to measure it would require a second absolute time external to this one against which you could compare it.

As mentioned above, Kant called time the form of inner sense. This is part of an interesting and fairly radical idea about the nature of time. He claimed that time was not a real feature of the world, but only the way that we organize our experience. To use some modern analogies, we typically think that the mind works the way a television set receives signals. A TV camera would be like our sense organs, picking up the sense data and transmitting them to the television set, which passively receives these signals in our consciousnesses, such that the sense information we receive is unaffected by the transmission process. But, according to the way Kant looks at things, the mind is more like a computer. It doesn't just passively register information about the world around us; rather, it actively processes information. Our senses are affected by objects in the world around us, and the mind takes those sense data, that information, and processes it in a particular way. One thing that it does in such processing is give a form or structure to that sense information. Part of that form or structure is time (also space, Kant argues). Consequently, beings with minds different from our own would experience the world quite differently, perhaps as not in time, since their minds might structure their sense data differently. God, for example, Kant says, does not experience the world as we do: as a temporal flow of events, the present ever sliding into the past, and the future always just on the horizon. God isn't subject to time, and so the notions of past, present, and future do not apply to God's experience.

A theory about time is part of what philosophers call metaphysics. Generally speaking, metaphysics is an understanding of the nature of reality, how the universe is put together. Newton's conception of absolute time says something about the nature of the world, as does Kant's idea that time is the form of inner sense.

There is a third idea about the nature of time and the nature of the universe that I want to focus on here. This is Friedrich Nietzsche's (1844–1900) conception of the eternal recurrence of the same. Nietzsche held the rather strange idea that all the events of our lives would return, would occur again and again throughout eternity. That is, this life, as we live it, each instant, we will have to live over and over again, an infinite number of times. There are different interpretations of what Nietzsche might have meant by this, whether he really believed it literally, and so forth. One thing is certain, though, and that is that Nietzsche considered the *thought* of the eternal recurrence to be something very serious. He called this thought "The Greatest Weight," and this is how he introduces it:

> *The greatest weight.* What, if some day or night a demon were to steal after you into your loneliest loneliness and say to you: "This life as you now live it and have lived it, you will have to live once more and innumerable times more; and there will be nothing new in it, but every pain and every joy and every thought and sigh and everything unutterably small or great in your life will have to return to you, all in the same succession and sequence—even this spider and this moonlight between the trees, and even this moment and I myself. The eternal hourglass of existence is turned upside down again and again, and you with it, speck of dust!"
>
> Would you not throw yourself down and gnash your teeth and curse the demon who spoke thus? Or have you once experienced a tremendous moment when you would have answered him: "You are a god and never have I heard anything more divine." If this thought gained possession of you, it would change you as your are or perhaps crush you. The question in each and every thing, "Do you desire this once more and innumerable times more?" would lie upon your actions as the greatest weight. Or how well disposed would you have to become to yourself and to life *to crave nothing more fervently* than this ultimate confirmation and seal?[3]

Imagine having to face your life as you live it an infinite number of times, with all its hardships and heartaches, pains, trials, and boredom. ("Great, that means I'll have to sit through the Ice Capades again," says Woody Allen in *Hannah and Her Sisters.*) Could any of us actually say that he or she would be willing to

---

[3] Friedrich Nietzsche, *The Gay Science,* section 341.

go through an infinitude of these lives? If not, then what are we doing with our lives? How are we living, what are we wasting our time with, if we cannot make this greatest of affirmations?

Notice that in this expression of the eternal recurrence, Nietzsche only says "*if*": "What, if some day or night a demon were to steal after you into your loneliest loneliness . . ." He doesn't at this point commit himself to saying that he thinks that this is true, that he's making an actual metaphysical claim. He's merely asking us to consider the thought of the eternal recurrence, what the effect of it would be on the way that we live our lives, and he's asking us to consider how it is that we are living our lives, if we cannot affirm the eternal recurrence of every aspect of those lives.

However, there is a second statement of the eternal recurrence in Nietzsche's writings. This is found in *Thus Spoke Zarathustra,* which is a narrative, a story about a prophet and teacher named Zarathustra. In the section called "On the Vision and the Riddle," Zarathustra and a dwarf companion, named the spirit of gravity, encounter the thought of the eternal recurrence. Notice that here, Nietzsche does not say "if." He seems here to be saying that this is an actual theory about the universe (but, ambiguously, he puts it in the mouth of a fictional character!).

"Behold this gateway, dwarf!" I continued. "It has two faces. Two paths meet here; no one has yet followed either to its end. This long lane stretches back for an eternity. And the long lane out there, that is another eternity. They contradict each other, these paths; they offend each other face to face; and it is here at this gateway that they come together. The name of the gateway is inscribed above: 'Moment' . . .

"Behold," I continued, "this moment! From this gateway, Moment, a long eternal lane leads *backwards*: behind us lies an eternity. Must not whatever can walk have walked on this lane before? Must not whatever *can* happen have happened, have been done, have passed by before? And if everything has been there before—what do you think, dwarf, of this moment? Must not this gateway too have been there before? And are not all things knotted together so firmly that this moment draws after it *all* that is to come? Therefore itself too? For whatever *can* walk—in this long lane out *there* too, it *must* walk once more.

"And this slow spider, which crawls in the moonlight, and this moonlight itself, and I and you in the gateway, whispering together, whispering of eternal things—must not all of us have been there before? And return and walk in that other lane, out there, before us, in this long dreadful lane—must we not eternally return?"[4]

Here Nietzsche connects the thought of the eternal recurrence to the notion of time. Zarathustra is standing in a gateway called "Moment"; in other words, he is standing in the present. But he sees an eternal lane stretching backwards, which is evidently the past. There is another eternal lane, which meets the past at the gateway. That, of course, must be the future. They contradict one another; they "offend each other face to face." And for some reason, Zarathustra thinks it's necessary that whatever can pass through the gateway, Moment, must have walked through that gateway somewhere along that eternal lane stretching backward, and indeed must walk through it again on the eternal lane stretching out in front.

In a moment I'll say more about Nietzsche's attempt to justify the eternal recurrence as an actual metaphysical claim, and not merely as a "what if." First, however, let's see what all this has to do with *Seinfeld*.

Recurrence in *Seinfeld*

It's clear that the various *Seinfeld* characters have experiences which continually recur, and some of them recur in exactly the same way, seemingly just as Nietzsche describes. For example, how many times have we seen Kramer slide through Jerry's door as an entrance? Dozens, surely. And how many times have we seen Jerry scowl, make a fist and through his clenched teeth utter "Newman!"? On many occasions we have seen Uncle Leo stretch out his arms and cry "Jerry! How are you?!" George often pretends to be an architect and calls himself Art Vandelay. How many bowls of cereal have we seen Jerry eat? How many cigars has Cosmo smoked? How many times have we vicariously had

---

[4] Friedrich Nietzsche, *Thus Spoke Zarathustra,* "On the Vision and the Riddle."

lunch at Monk's? These are actions that recur continually for
these characters, in exactly the same way.

On the other hand, there are many other actions and situations that recur, which aren't exactly identical, but which are the
same in spirit. These too are recurrences. How many women
has Jerry broken up with or lost for trivial reasons? She has man
hands; she had her breasts done; she found out Jerry was in a
contest with his friends to see who could go the longest without self-gratification; he becomes fixated on her toy collection;
she's a cashier but doesn't respect what he does for a living; she
likes a Dockers pants commercial that he hates; he can't remember her name; her toothbrush fell in the toilet; she has a tube of
fungicide in her medicine cabinet; she thought she caught Jerry
picking his nose; she eats peas one at a time with a fork; she
got gonorrhea from a tractor; he can't help but make a funny
voice that he imagines is the sound of her stomach talking; she
was perfect in his eyes (and his parents'—that's the clincher),
but everyone else saw her as a loser; she's exactly like him; she
only wears one outfit.

Then there's George. What are his recurring experiences? His
inability to keep a job, surely. And the fact that he gets fired or
quits for strange reasons. He has sex with the cleaning woman;
his boss won't let him use the executive wash room; he gets
traded from the Yankees to a chicken company. He also blows
job prospects for odd reasons: he meets a beautiful woman on
a subway and follows her instead of going to a scheduled second interview; unfortunately she robs him and leaves him hand-
cuffed to a bed in a hotel room. On another occasion, George
has an interview for a job selling bras, but finds himself in trouble when he feels the jacket fabric of a woman who turns out
to be the boss. He also has recurring conflicts with his parents.
Many times we hear Estelle's shrill voice drowned out by Frank's
over-the-top yelling, while George grimaces and buries his head
in his hands.

Kramer's wild and always abortive schemes recur. He and
Newman gather bottles and return them to Michigan in a postal
van to collect the deposits. He designs a rubber lining for
tankers to avoid oil spills in the ocean. He tries to import
Cubans to roll cigars for him. He helps to refurbish a theater.
Imitating Leonardo da Vinci, he sleeps only a few hours a night,
with disastrous effects. When J. Peterman publishes a book of

Kramer's exploits, claiming them for his own, Cosmo starts "The Real Peterman Reality Tour." He goes into the raincoat business with Morty Seinfeld. He plans for a millennium party and wonders if people will be able to breathe under water in the year two thousand. Angry at the Pottery Barn for all the catalogues he receives, Kramer starts an anti-mail campaign. He wants to run the neighborhood Kenny Rogers Roasters out of business. A number of times he turns to the lawyer Jackie Chiles with a get-rich-quick lawsuit.

Elaine has recurring man troubles. One boyfriend broke up with her because she stopped off for jujyfruits before coming to see him at the hospital. She got involved with her manipulative psychiatrist, and had a hard time getting out of his clutches. She became the object of affection of Crazy Joe Davola, a psychopathic opera fan. She stirs up trouble when she tries to get a boyfriend to change his name from Joel Rifkin, because he shares that name with a serial killer. She falls for a gay man and tries to get him to "switch teams," as it were. She breaks up with an artist, because he is too fat; he gets sick, loses weight, and she finds herself attracted to him again. But when he gets better, she anticipates that he will get fat again, and so she loses interest once more. She is continually getting together with and breaking up with David Puddy, a less than intelligent auto mechanic (and then salesman) and face-painting hockey fan.

Yes, the *Seinfeldians* have experiences that recur. Some of those recurrences are exactly the same, and others are the same in spirit. Is this what Nietzsche had in mind? Well, no, it doesn't seem so. These are only individual actions and sequences that recur, while the situations and settings vary. In other words, while Nietzsche said that every instant would return in exactly the same way, such that one would have the same life from beginning to end repeated over and over, in the *Seinfeld* world we are not witnessing the repetition of whole lives. Rather, within the one lifetime (which lasted nine seasons), we saw the recurrence of these various themes and actions. If we had a true recurrence, I suppose, that would mean watching the same episode over and over again—or, better, what it would mean would be to take all nine seasons' worth of episodes and run them continuously from first to last over and over again. This does happen in syndication, of course, but this is not what we have in mind here. The question is not why are the episodes continually repeated in syndication (which is answered easily enough), but rather: why do these things keep happening to these characters, internally, as it were, within the history of the show? Why do the same or similar things keep happening within the series?

The clue to answering this can be found in a more complete explanation of why a Nietzschean explanation fails here. Nietzsche believed that the world, the universe, was a flux, a never stable, never ending, continually changing flux. In a series of notes, collected after his death and titled *The Will to Power,* Nietzsche gives a quasi-scientific explanation for the eternal recurrence. He says:

> If the world may be thought of as a certain definite quantity of force and as a certain definite number of centers of force . . . it follows that, in the great dice game of existence, it must pass through a calculable number of combinations. In infinite time, every possible combination would at some time or another be realized; more: it would be realized an infinite number of times. And since between every combination and its next recurrence all other possible combinations would have to take place, and each of these combinations conditions the entire sequence of combinations in the same series, a circular movement of absolutely identical series is thus demonstrated: the world as a circular movement that has already repeated itself infinitely often plays its game *in infinitum.*[5]

The universe consists in "centers of force," the ever shifting, ever changing components of the flux. The universe is finite, and so the number of centers of force is necessarily finite. These centers of force come together and combine with one another to make up the objects that we experience in the world—people, trees, planets, non-fat yogurt, Buicks, and so on. But the centers of force don't stay in any one combination for any long period of time (in the grand scheme of things). They thus decompose, only to recombine with other centers of force in other combinations. This is what the universe is or consists in: this continual combining and re-combining of centers of force. Now, since

---

[5] Friedrich Nietzsche, *The Will to Power,* Section 1066.

the number of centers of force is finite, given that the universe is finite, if the universe is eternal, that is, has lasted forever, and will last forever, every possible combination of centers of force will have to be run through, and indeed in infinite time it will be run through an infinite number of times. Consequently, the combination of centers of force that constitutes you or me has already been in this configuration and will be so again in the future an infinite number of times.

It's not clear how seriously Nietzsche took this quasi-scientific explanation, given that he never published it himself. Again, it only appears in his notes. It is easily shown that the explanation doesn't hold water. It is possible to show that, with as few as three variables, and in infinite time, the same combinations of those variables would never have to recur. For our purposes, though, that's not important. The key to our questions about the *Seinfeld* universe is the fact that Nietzsche took the world to be an ever-changing flux. There is no doubt that he believed this; the expression of that idea is found throughout his published works.

If Nietzsche holds a flux metaphysics, then we are definitely barking up the wrong tree in our attempt to explain the *Seinfeld* universe philosophically. The *Seinfeld* universe cannot be explicated in terms of an ever-shifting flux of power centers. No, it is in fact the opposite. Things recur in the *Seinfeld* universe not because everything continually changes. Things recur there precisely because *nothing changes!*

Plato and the Changing vs. the Unchanging

We've stumbled here upon a classic philosophical issue, change and stability. In the West, this issue goes back at least to the ancient Greeks. The question or the issue is: how do we make sense of the fact that the world around us changes, is in flux, while certain things seem to stay the same? How do we explain the unchanging within the apparently ever-changing world? Some of the ancient Greek philosophers also touched upon the role that sense perception plays in our understanding of the universe, versus the role played by reason. In other words, our senses seem to tell us that the world is forever changing, while reason is able to tap into realities (like numbers, for instance) which never change.

Let me quickly sketch one response to this problem, before moving on to a second, which I believe is the one we want. Parmenides was an ancient Greek philosopher who solved the change versus stability issue by eliminating change. A contemporary philosopher explains Parmenides' view thus:

> [Parmenides'] doctrine in brief is to the effect that Being, the One, is, and that Becoming, change, is illusion. For if anything comes to be, then it comes either out of being or out of non-being. If the former, then it already is—in which case it does not come to be; if the latter, then it is nothing, since out of nothing comes nothing. Becoming is, then, illusion.[6]

Parmenides trusted reason over the testimony of the senses, and thus made metaphysics into the kind of problem that could be solved with logic. He identified that which exists, that which is, as being, and that which does not exist as non-being, or nothing. Given these two categories, being and non-being, Parmenides reasoned that there simply is no room for change or becoming (coming to be). That is, if something comes to be, if it changes from one thing into another, then it must come to be either from being, that which already is in existence, or from non-being, nothingness. But being, that which is, already *is*, and thus doesn't come to be. And nothing doesn't do anything at all; it's simply nothing.[7] Consequently, logically, change is impossible, and thus an illusion. This is a radical conclusion, and it contradicts what our senses tell us about the world. But when the senses come into conflict with reason, Parmenides argued, reason must prevail.

Plato also addressed the problem of the changing versus the unchanging, and clearly he was influenced by Parmenides. Before we examine Plato's metaphysics, however, let's first discuss the relationship between Plato and Socrates. Socrates was Plato's teacher and, to say the least, was a very interesting

---

[6] Frederick Copleston, S.J., *History of Philosophy,* Vol. 1, "Greece and Rome," p. 48.

[7] For an interesting discussion of nothing see Eric Bronson's "Making Something out of Nothing: *Seinfeld,* Sophistry, and the Tao," in this volume.

figure. There is much about him that is eccentric and unusual. For example, though he was a great philosopher, he never wrote anything. Socrates confined his philosophy to thinking about things and arguing with others; he never committed his thoughts to paper, but rather, to some extent, expressed them in his actions. Plato, on the other hand, was a prolific writer of philosophical treatises. The majority of these works that have survived are narratives, stories, called dialogues, and the main character of these dialogues in most cases is Socrates. Consequently, it's often difficult to separate out what Socrates thought from what Plato thought.[8] Fortunately, for present purposes, that is not important. Let's just make note of this historical and methodological fact. Keep in mind in the passages we shall discuss, that it is Socrates (supposedly) speaking, but that it is Plato who is doing the writing.

Like Parmenides, Plato favored reason over the testimony of the senses. He believed that it is the mind that allows us to understand ultimate reality, while the senses very often deceive us. But unlike Parmenides, Plato didn't go so far as to declare change to be a complete illusion. He did take it to be axiomatic that what is ultimately real is unchanging. Now, given that the everyday world of plants and animals around us does in fact change, it follows that this everyday world is not ultimate reality. While not a complete illusion, this everyday world is less real. Less real than what? Plato makes a sharp division between two kinds of reality, or two worlds. There is the changing world of things, or what he called particulars, and there is the unchanging world of Forms. The one world is accessible through sense perception, and the other world is accessible through the mind and reason.

> SOCRATES: Do we say that there is such a thing as the Just itself, or not?
>
> SIMMIAS: We do say so, by Zeus.
>
> SOCRATES: And the Beautiful, and the Good?
>
> SIMMIAS: Of course.

---

[8] For a discussion of this problem see William Irwin's "Jerry and Socrates: The Examined Life?" in this volume.

SOCRATES: And have you ever seen any of these things with your eyes?

SIMMIAS: In no way . . .

SOCRATES: Or have you ever grasped them with any of your bodily senses? I am speaking of all things such as Size, Health, Strength and, in a word, the reality of all other things, that which each of them essentially is. Is what is most true in them contemplated through the body, or is this the position: whoever of us prepares himself best and most accurately to grasp that thing itself which he is investigating will come closest to the knowledge of it?

SIMMIAS: Obviously.

SOCRATES: Then he will do this most perfectly who approaches the object with thought alone, without associating any sight with his thought, or dragging in any sense perception with his reasoning, but who, using pure thought alone, tries to track down each reality pure and by itself, freeing himself as far as possible from eyes and ears, and in a word, from the whole body, because the body confuses the soul . . .[9]

Plato declared that for all the individual, particular things we see, touch, hear, taste and feel in the world around us, there is some unchanging model, or Form, which makes those things what they are. For example, there are many individual, particular chairs that exist in the world, in space and time, and which come into existence and go out of existence. Now, what do these particulars have in common, how is it that they all fall into the same class or category? Plato argues that they are all copied after one and the same Form, a perfect and unchanging model which is not perceptible, not sensible, but which is rather intelligible; it is knowable. That is, particulars exist in space and time; they are sensible, corruptible, finite, changing. Forms, on the other hand, are unchanging, atemporal, aspatial, eternal models of things.

---

[9] Plato, *Phaedo*, 65d.

Plato doesn't generally talk about things like desks or people. In the passage above, he mentions justice, beauty, and goodness. He is more interested in these kinds of things. The point is that in the everyday world of particulars there are beautiful things and just actions. Our being able to identify things in the world as beautiful and just, Plato says, is only possible because there is a perfect standard or Form of beauty and justice. In the *Republic*, he says:

SOCRATES: Since the beautiful is the opposite of the ugly, they are two.

GLAUCON: Of course.

SOCRATES: And since they are two, each is one?

GLAUCON: I grant that also.

SOCRATES: And the same is true of the just and the unjust, the good and the bad, and all the Forms. Each of them is itself one, but because they manifest themselves everywhere in association with actions, bodies, and one another, each of them appears to be many.

GLAUCON: That's right.[10]

The beautiful, in other words, the Form of beauty is singular and unchanging. It is one thing, but it manifests itself in association with actions and body; it appears in the world around us as many particular beautiful things.

Plato's theory of Forms is one of the first well-developed theories of *essences*. What is an essence? Well, it is what makes a thing what it is and not another thing. If I ask, what is my essence, it is surely human being—that's my nature, it is what makes me who and what I am. If I ask what is the essence of the wooden thing in front of me on which my computer sits, I answer that it is a desk. That is what makes it what it is and not another thing. What Plato noticed was that particular examples of things come and go—desks are made, they exist for a while, and they are destroyed—but the essences of these things

---

[10] Plato, *Republic*, 475e–476a.

remain. This is why he took the physical, material particulars to be less real than the Forms: that which is ultimately real is lasting; it endures.

This essay began with a quote from Nietzsche regarding music. Let's return to that theme for a moment. When explaining Plato's theory of Forms, I like to use an analogy to music. Think of a piece of music. I usually mention the fourth movement to Beethoven's Ninth Symphony, but if you'd rather think of Milli Vanilli, feel free. Now, what are the different ways in which you can experience this particular piece of music? You could listen to a tape or a CD; hear it in a concert hall; read the sheet music; perform it yourself; whistle, hum, or sing it. The question is, what is the symphony? Is it equal to any particular copy or performance of it? If the CD breaks, does the symphony suddenly disappear? If it is performed badly, or if the performance is interrupted, has the symphony changed? If all copies of it were destroyed, and if it weren't being performed, has it suddenly vanished, been obliterated? The answer to all of these questions is no, of course not. The symphony somehow transcends any particular example or copy of it. While the individual copies and performances come and go, while they have finite duration, beginnings and endings, the symphony itself somehow endures. It remains unchanged. Further, the symphony, whatever that thing is, is the essence of all the different examples of it—it is what makes them what they are, copies or performances *of the Ninth Symphony.* In this analogy, of course, the different recordings and performances are Plato's particulars, while the symphony itself is the Form.

To make the analogy between music and humor once more, notice that what we said about the symphony above can be applied to a joke. Jokes can be told and retold ("They only eat fish"), and they can be told better and worse. We could say that this means that the joke has a kind of essence that transcends any particular telling of it, and it is this essence which makes any particular telling a telling *of this joke.* Because there is this essence to the joke, we can say that a version of it is better or worse—it acts as a kind of standard by which to judge. "You blew the punch line," we can say, since this particular instance of the joke failed to match the essence of the joke; it was an imperfect copy of the transcendent essence.

The *Seinfeldians* as Fixed Essences

To return to the main argument, then, we noticed that the *Seinfeldians* have their recurring experiences, and we realized that this is not because of Nietzschean eternal recurrence, since Nietzsche conceived of the universe as a flux, as continually changing. As we noticed, the reason that there is recurrence in the *Seinfeld* universe is precisely because nothing changes. What I want to claim is that, like the symphony or like a joke in the analogies I employed, Jerry, George, Kramer, and Elaine have fixed essences. The *Seinfeld* universe is one made up of Platonic-like Forms which stand outside time. We then see these Platonic *Seinfeld* Forms manifested in the flow of time that is the show. Jerry will forever be the fastidious comedian who changes girlfriends like the rest of us change shirts. George is the anxiety-ridden underachiever, full of guilt and forever under-confident. Elaine is the everyday, girl next door, somewhat shallow, a little bitter, and always in search of a man. And Kramer is . . . well, he's *Kramer.*

That the *Seinfeldians* are fixed characters is interestingly shown in "The Bizarro Jerry." This is the episode in which Elaine stumbles onto the *Seinfeld* Bizarro world, in which Jerry, George, and Kramer have their exact opposites. The Bizarro world is centered around Jerry's opposite, Kevin. His apartment looks just like Jerry's, except that, from right to left, everything is arranged exactly the reverse of Jerry's place. In this world, Kevin, Gene (George's opposite), and Feldman (Kramer's opposite) have in-depth and meaningful conversations about interesting and important topics, even talking about *useful* inventions which they've thought of. They read books, and Kramer's reverse doppelganger knocks on his neighbor's door before entering (after identifying himself as "Feldman—from across the hall" each and every time) and fills Kevin's refrigerator, rather than emptying it. They are courteous to one another, and they go to the ballet. Even Newman has his opposite, Vargas, who gets along with Kevin (Jerry's opposite) and is not a mailman, but rather works for one of the package delivery companies—the direct competition of the U.S. Postal Service.

Now, the very fact that Jerry, George, and Kramer have their exact opposites tells us that they themselves are fixed character types. Instead of being ever-changing, dynamic complexes of a

Nietzschean variety, who could not have direct and exact opposites, given their fluid natures, the *Seinfeldians* are fixed, never-
changing archetypes. Instead of being characters who, subject to
time and change, develop through experience and reflection,
and who learn from their mistakes, maturing and growing, the
Seinfeld quartet (and extended family) is seemingly isolated from
time and change. They are Platonic-like Forms, essences which
are not subject to the vicissitudes of the world in any real way,
and which are exempt from the terrible march of time. And as
these archetypes, as these Forms or essences, the *Seinfeld* four
can and do have their direct opposites in the eerie Bizarro world
where manners, thoughtfulness, and culture prevail. To repeat,
that which changes can have no real opposite. Only that which
does not change can have its true reverse reflection shown to it.

At the beginning of this essay, we saw that time is a central
human concern and a philosophical problem. Our lives are
arranged around the incessant flow of time and the fact that we
are finite creatures—the fact that we only have so much time.
The future rushes towards us, the present disappears in an
instant and flows into the ever-increasing infinity of the past. We
plan for the future, and often we dwell in the past, in the sense
of replaying our memories or pining over lost loves and unful-
filled expectations. But time only moves in one direction for us.
It is a moving walkway carrying us inevitably and invariably
toward death's dateless night.

It is different for the denizens of the *Seinfeld* universe. They
have a vastly different relationship to time, and this can be seen
in the final season's backward episode ("The Betrayal"). At the
"beginning" of this episode, we see Jerry, George, and Elaine
returning from some kind of trip to India (of all places). They
are angry with one another, and apparently the trip has been
something of a fiasco. As we progress backwards through the
events leading up to the return home, we discover the reasons
for their foul moods and their quarrels. Elaine had been invited
to Sue Ellen Mishki's wedding in India and had accepted out of
spite. As it turns out, Elaine had slept with Pintar, the groom,
sometime previously, and the discovery of this fact ruined the
wedding. In addition Jerry had slept with George's date, Nina.
Adding to his troubles, George had been wearing the same pair
of boots the whole time to make himself look taller in front of
Nina, and he had refused to go to the bathroom away from

home, thus causing himself great personal distress. (No apologies for this. "You can stuff your sorries in a sack!") There is a sub-plot involving Kramer. At the start of the half-hour, we see him concluding a feud with F.D.R. (Franklin Delano Romanowski) over a bizarre series of wish-makings, and as the show proceeds we learn the details of the feud and how it began.

The fact that the characters are fixed archetypes or essences which never change means that time is irrelevant to them. Since they never grow or change or develop, the direction that time and events take in their lives, whether backward or forward, makes no difference at all. We can start at the end and end at the beginning, for beginnings and endings are only relative reference points in a flow of actions and events to which the *Seinfeld* character archetypes are not subject.

Backwards or forwards, past, present, or future—none of these matter. We know that Kramer will always have another wild scheme, and that he will come sliding through the door to Jerry's apartment; George will forever lack confidence and will forever have difficulty holding a job; Elaine will continue to date and break up with David Puddy, all the while hoping to meet someone more intelligent and successful; Jerry will invariably continue to find some petty reason to break up with his girlfriends, and he will continue to struggle with his nemesis, Newman. These are constants in an otherwise ever-changing and thus merciless universe. Yes, *Seinfeld* has solved the problem of time, and there's something very comforting about that.

7
Seinfeld, Subjectivity, and Sartre

JENNIFER McMAHON

From its initial airing to its final episode, the sitcom *Seinfeld* captured the hearts and minds of millions of viewers. Though *Seinfeld* purports to be *about nothing,* its remarkable success demonstrates that the program strikes *something* with the viewing public. One thing that *Seinfeld* seems to have hit upon is a truth about friendship. Most people have friends. Friends are individuals with whom we share our time, our dreams, and even our insecurities. Friends are indispensable sources of support in our times of need. They are the ones whose company we seek in times of joy. We cherish our friends in large part because we feel we can be ourselves with them. It is my contention that we not only share ourselves with our friends, but that our *selves* are structured by our friendships. Our friends contribute to making us who we are. Our friends affect us in indelible ways. We would not be the same without them. The sitcom *Seinfeld* illustrates this point clearly. The characters in *Seinfeld* mutually define one another. Neither Jerry, George, Kramer, nor Elaine could be neatly separated out from the mix. They need each other to be who they are.

In the following, I shall argue that *Seinfeld* serves to illustrate the fact that personal identity is established relationally. An analysis of the characters in *Seinfeld* reveals that interactions with others are essential to the consolidation of a self. Throughout history, the self has been a topic of debate. For centuries philosophers have pondered the nature of this odd entity.

Though philosophers have tended to adopt the position that the self has some essential and autonomous core, alternative theories have garnered support recently. These theories deny the essentiality and autonomy of the self. They maintain that the self is something created through intersubjective activity. In an effort to bolster my claims about *Seinfeld* and the role that friends play in the formation of self, I shall draw from existentialist philosopher Jean-Paul Sartre's theory of subjectivity. I shall argue that what Sartre and *Seinfeld* reveal is that we find our selves in our relations with others. I shall suggest that what *Seinfeld* does more effectively than Sartre is demonstrate the positive role that friends play in identity formation.

Addressing the Skeptics or "Get Out!
Seinfeld as Philosophy?"

Admittedly, my claims about *Seinfeld* and Sartre may surprise some readers. There are two major reasons why this is the case. The first is obvious. Certainly, some readers will think it a stretch to claim that a sitcom like *Seinfeld* could say anything expressly philosophical about the self. Second, readers familiar with Sartre's work and Sartre scholarship may wonder how a philosopher so suspicious of social relations can be seen as being an advocate of a relational theory of the self. Like Elaine, some readers may respond incredulously, "Get out!!!," when confronted with the claim that *Seinfeld* and Sartre illustrate the philosophic point that the individual needs others to have a fully formed and functional self. Thus, before I turn my attention to elaborating precisely what *Seinfeld* and Sartre can tell us about the self, I would like to try and address these concerns.

First, let me address the question of how a television sitcom like *Seinfeld* could provide information of legitimate philosophic interest. Undoubtedly, some people regard television viewing—particularly the viewing of television sitcoms—as an effort on the part of the individual viewer to find a temporary mental escape from the stresses of ordinary reality. Simply put, some people view sitcoms as thirty-minute respites from everyday life. While these individuals recognize sitcoms as forms of entertainment, they are skeptical with respect to the potential that sitcoms have to educate. Though they would accept that sitcoms can make us laugh, they would be reluctant to admit that they can also help us learn. Ultimately, the suspicion of the instructive ability of sitcoms rests on two illegitimate assumptions. The first is that we cannot learn from fiction. The second is that levity and learning are mutually exclusive.

The belief that we cannot learn from fiction has been around for centuries. Indeed, ever since Plato declared that exposure to fiction distorted peoples' understanding and corrupted their moral character, philosophers have debated whether fiction could provide any legitimate form of knowledge. Today, the philosophical debate about fiction centers on the question of how works of *fiction* (such as novels, films, sitcoms) could offer individuals *factual* information. Those skeptical of the instructive abilities of fiction argue that it is logically impossible for works about characters or situations that are *not real* to provide individuals with pertinent information about the *real* world.

The problem with the skeptical analysis is twofold. First, it presumes too radical a separation between fact and fiction. Second, it ignores the fact that people have been using stories as a means to educate for hundreds—indeed thousands—of years. Centuries of success ought to count for something. Though there is certainly a difference between fact and fiction, between real people and the ones we see on "Must See TV," the difference is not so great as to preclude us learning from fictional characters or events. While *unreal* in the obvious physical sense, our favorite fictional characters and events are generally the ones that impress us with their *realness*. Successful fictions resonate with us. They tell us something about reality. Through the characters and situations they present, works of fiction offer us useful insights about human nature, ourselves, or our times.

Here, the characters and situations presented in *Seinfeld* serve as excellent examples. One of the reasons for *Seinfeld*'s success is the fact that viewers see a bit of themselves in the sitcom. After all, who doesn't know someone who is crazy like Kramer, or cynical like George? Who hasn't seen themselves in Jerry or Elaine? Whether we like it or not, there are people like Crazy Joe Davola, the Soup Nazi, and Newman in our lives. Like Jerry, George, Kramer, and Elaine, we know *close-talkers* and *sentence-finishers*. Each of us has had our share of inane experiences and absurd conversations. Most of us have spent more time than we'd like to admit hanging out in friends' apartments and coffee shops. Albeit in caricatured form, *Seinfeld* offers viewers a reflection of everyday life in the nineties. Like each member of the *Seinfeld* gang, our everyday lives are comprised primarily of events and annoyances we consider too ordinary to inspire much interest. Apart from the occasional momentous event, one could say that our lives are also *about nothing.* *Seinfeld* reminds us how interesting and amusing everyday life can be. It helps restore our appreciation of the commonplace, of the million ordinary moments that together make up our lives. Far from transporting viewers into a field of fantasy, the success of the sitcom *Seinfeld* lies in the way it shows us—and make us smile at—ourselves.

Of course, one of the reasons *Seinfeld* is so successful at conveying its image of life to viewers is its ability to make viewers smile. Though there are still those who would contend that information has to be conveyed in a serious manner in order to be conveyed effectively, this assumption is not only without foundation, it betrays a pernicious intellectual elitism. Whether it offends one's intellectual taste or not, humor is an incredible pedagogical tool. Though serious speaking and writing will always have their place, they are not the only means of getting a message across. In the case of *Seinfeld,* the sitcom's humor suits the subject matter it presents. A comic phenomenology, *Seinfeld* offers its viewers an image of contemporary life. Though we tend to take our lives and ourselves pretty seriously, most of us will admit that life is incredibly funny at times. Each of our lives is filled with an abundance of trips, falls, mishaps and misadventures, embarrassing mis-statements and unforgettable funnies. The sort of life depicted by a sober *Seinfeld* would probably not be one most of us would recognize.

Though it may sound like a whole lot of *yada yada yada* to some, hopefully the contents of the previous paragraphs are enough to convince those skeptical of the instructive ability of fiction that even funny fictions like *Seinfeld* can offer individuals information that is of real interest and significance. However, when considering the initial plausibility of my claims about *Seinfeld,* Sartre and the self, one question remains. The question pertains to Sartre. Admittedly, those familiar with Sartre's work and Sartre criticism may wonder how I can claim that Sartre is an advocate of a relational theory of the self. Indeed, Sartre's suspicion of social relations and his well-known declaration, "Hell is other people,"[1] would seem to make him an unlikely supporter of the notion that others are essential to the formation of the self. Though Sartre has been pegged by most critics as a dualist whose ontology preserves an essentialist understanding of the self, these interpretations result from misunderstanding Sartre's definition of consciousness and the nature of his distinction between consciousness and the world.

Sartre on the Subject

Until recently, essentialist understandings of the self were the norm in philosophy. Indeed, some of the most famous figures in philosophy have asserted that there is some essential or core self. For centuries, the tendency in philosophy has been to characterize the self as something independent of experience, unaffected by others, and impervious to material influence. However, as a result of the increasing amount of evidence supplied by research in the physical and social sciences, philosophers have begun to alter their understanding of the self. More and more, philosophers have come to regard personal identity as something that depends upon a host of experiential factors. Instead of seeing the self as an essential and autonomous entity, an increasing number of philosophers have come to regard subjectivity as something that emerges within a social and historical framework.

Sartre can be seen as a representative of this sort of relational theory of the self. In *Being and Nothingness,* Sartre offers his understanding of existence in exacting detail. One of the most important claims that Sartre makes in this text is that there is a radical distinction between consciousness and the world of which it is aware. Unfortunately, this claim has led many of Sartre's critics to assert that an essentialist understanding of the self is implicit in Sartre's ontology. These critics argue that by distinguishing consciousness from the world of experience, Sartre has established an essential, nonexperiential, and nonre-

---

[1] Jean-Paul Sartre, *No Exit,* in *No Exit* and *The Flies* (New York: Knopf, 1954), p. 61.

lational basis for the self. The problem with this analysis is that while Sartre does think it necessary to recognize a distinction between consciousness and the world, it does not follow from this that he has committed himself to an essentialist conception of the subject. Instead, when one analyzes Sartre's theory of consciousness and how it relates to subjectivity carefully, it becomes apparent that he could advocate nothing other than a relational conception of the self.

The theory of consciousness that Sartre offers in *Being and Nothingness* is not particularly easy to understand. It is a conceptual masterpiece, but it is also replete with complex terminology and cast in nearly impenetrable prose. Since its publication in 1943, it has inspired as much frustration as fascination. Without question, what has confounded Sartre's readers the most is his claim that consciousness is a nothingness. Certainly, this claim seems odd. Consciousness is something we experience. It is something we have. It does not seem to make sense to say that consciousness is nothing. Ultimately, Sartre uses the term nothingness to describe consciousness because he feels that this particular term is able to capture several important phenomenological features of our awareness.

The main thing that the term nothingness does is draw our attention to the difference that exists between consciousness and its objects. According to Sartre, there is a necessary gap between consciousness and the world. He asserts that if we examine consciousness carefully we find that consciousness is predicated on a subject/object distinction. Simply put, Sartre argues that in order for *consciousness of* a particular object to exist, consciousness *must not be* that object. In the same way that the eye is separate from what it sees, Sartre argues that consciousness must be separate from its objects in order to have awareness of them. Since all *beings* or existing things are potential objects of consciousness, Sartre sees it necessary to characterize consciousness metaphorically as a *non-being*, or nothingness.

A second reason that Sartre uses the term nothingness to describe consciousness is because consciousness is not a *thing* in the way that chairs and tables are. Unlike most *things*, consciousness is notoriously difficult to grasp. It is elusive. It isn't something that we can get our hands on in the way we can get our hands on a ball or a book. With the term nothingness, Sartre makes the paradoxical nature of consciousness clear. Though it is consciousness that gives us an awareness of things in the world, consciousness itself has *no-thingness*. By utilizing the term nothingness, Sartre is able to convey the unique intangibility of consciousness more effectively.

The final—and for our purposes most important—reason that Sartre uses the term nothingness to characterize consciousness is to make it clear that consciousness is neither an indication of, nor synonymous with, an essential or otherworldly self. Though Sartre thinks it necessary to recognize that a gap exists between consciousness and the world of experience, the separation that he identifies is simply the distance necessary for awareness. It should not be taken as a suggestion that consciousness is some essential entity. For Sartre, consciousness is something that exists in the world. He utilizes the term nothingness in connection with consciousness to emphasize that consciousness is *not something* that exists in a realm apart from experience. In Sartre's opinion, the world of experience is all that there is. There is nothing outside existence, no essences, no other realms.

Ironically, though one of the main reasons that Sartre characterizes consciousness as a nothingness is to reinforce his belief that consciousness is *nothing* other than the awareness that a concrete individual has of the world, this is not how he is interpreted normally. Instead, in most of the secondary literature, critics have taken Sartre's claim that consciousness is a nothingness to mean that consciousness is independent of the world of experience and equivalent to an essential self. However, a careful analysis shows these assessments to be inaccurate.

Throughout *Being and Nothingness,* Sartre makes it clear that consciousness is situated. Far from being an autonomous free-floating entity, Sartre asserts that consciousness is inseparable from "its situation."[2] He indicates that consciousness occurs exclusively in the world and states explicitly that consciousness can only occur in connection with a living body.

Sartre also asserts in *Being and Nothingness* that there is no such thing as an essential self. Though he acknowledges that

---

[2] Jean-Paul Sartre, *Being and Nothingness* (New York: Washington Square Press, 1956), p. 702. Further references to this work will be indicated in parentheses by *BN* accompanied by page numbers.

such things as selves exist, he finds the idea of an essential subject so implausible that he devotes the whole of *Transcendence
of the Ego* to refuting the existence of such an entity. According
to Sartre, a self is something that an individual develops through
the course of her experience. It neither precedes the individual,
nor persists after her death. It is linked, but not equivalent to
consciousness. Consciousness is a necessary condition for the
self's emergence, but consciousness alone is not sufficient to
establish it. As Sartre explains, consciousness cannot be equated
with identity because all that consciousness *is* is bare experiential awareness. It is *nothing* other than the awareness that the
individual has of the world. It is *nothing* like what we call a self.

In order to have a self, Sartre asserts that the individual needs
others. He contends that corporeal and linguistic interactions
with others "[are] the necessary condition of all thought which I
would attempt to form concerning myself" (*BN*, p. 362). In
Sartre's estimation, personal identity is not something that exists
independent of others. Rather, it is something that emerges
within a social context.

The reason that the consolidation of self requires the input
of others is because the individual is incapable of developing an
objective sense of herself without assistance. Ultimately, a self is
an idea, a concept that is formulated reflexively. What it means
to have a self is to possess a sense of oneself as an object, or
thing. To have a self is to apprehend oneself as an entity with
concrete characteristics, definitive aims and aversions. A sense
of self is essential to the individual because it makes it possible
for the individual to make informed choices. Imagine trying to
make a decision about a career if one had no sense of self, no
sense of personal aptitudes and interests, no sense of personal
dislikes and incapacities. It would be impossible. A sense of self
guides an individual in her decision-making. Though individuals need selves, they cannot develop them in isolation.
According to Sartre, individuals cannot develop selves indepen-
dently because the consciousness that enlivens their corporeal
frames resists objectification.

In *Being and Nothingness,* Sartre emphasizes that consciousness is not a thing. Instead, he indicates that consciousness's
ability to afford awareness *of* things stems from the fact that it is
noncoincidental with them. Simply put, consciousness's "seeing"
is predicated on separation from the "seen." The development

of a sense of self demands the presence and participation of others because others are the only ones that can make the individual fully apprehend her objectness. According to Sartre, individuals are unique composites of consciousness and body. Though individuals are not unaware of their object-aspect (for example, their bodies, appearance, and dispositions) in the absence of others, their consciousness is such that it makes them feel subtly but essentially separate from their material nature. This sounds a bit strange, but a moment of reflection confirms this insight. For example, think of the times one has caught the reflection of oneself in a window and felt somehow disconnected from that reflection. Think of the times one has looked at one's hand, or one's face in the mirror, and thought "That is not me." According to Sartre, though consciousness could not exist outside the objective situation of embodiment, it nonetheless cannot help but experience itself as not-object. As such, it is the nature of our consciousness to make us feel not quite coincidental with our embodied experience.

Because of the nature of consciousness, others need to be present in order for an individual to consolidate a sense of self. Sartre states, "the Other accomplishes for us a function of which we are incapable and which nevertheless is incumbent upon us: to see ourselves as we are" (*BN,* p. 463). We need others because it is exclusively through our interactions with them that we come to understand and accept our objective nature. According to Sartre, we don't have selves when we start out. Instead, selves develop reflexively in response to our relations with others. In Sartre's estimation, an individual's sense of self emerges as she assimilates or begins to identify with the roles or characterizations that others have ascribed to her. Sartre asserts that selves are created from the internalization of information that social relations provide. He maintains that our selves are continually influenced and altered by our relationships. According to Sartre, from the time we are small children, we look to others to learn not only about the world, but about ourselves. We search others' eyes and analyze their comments in an effort to glean information about who we are. Sartre believes that our interactions with others are the living mirrors that keep us continually informed of our selves.

Though French philosophers and NBC sitcoms might not seem to have much in common, Sartre and *Seinfeld* offer surprisingly similar accounts of the self. Ultimately, both Sartre and *Seinfeld* demonstrate that personal identity emerges in a relational context. Interestingly, what *Seinfeld* does more effectively than Sartre is show how the particular relationship of friendship serves to influence the formation of self.

Seinfeld and the Role Friends Play in the Formation of the Self

In *Being and Nothingness,* Sartre presents his theory that interactions with others are essential to the formation of self. Because Sartre's objective is to make a point about the role that others play in identity formation generally, he draws readers' attention to others as a class. He focuses on the influence of others in a general sense, not on the influence of individual others. Obviously however, others are individuals. Though it is true that we need others—in general—to develop selves, there are different types of others, and these types affect the development of self differently. *Seinfeld* illustrates this point and tells us something about the importance of a particular group of others. It informs us of the significance of friends.

As successfully as Sartre, *Seinfeld* reveals that an individual can only develop a self within a social context. The way that *Seinfeld* demonstrates this is by illustrating the inseparability of the identities of individual characters from the network of friends that these characters comprise. When one considers the characters in *Seinfeld*, it hardly makes sense to talk about them as anything but a unit. The identities of Jerry, George, Kramer, and Elaine are inescapably intertwined. Far from having discrete and impervious *selves*, the characters on *Seinfeld* define one another. The identities of both the main and supporting characters are structured by their relationships. The removal of any single character would affect the identities of the remaining ones.

The focus of *Seinfeld* is the life of the character/comedian Jerry Seinfeld. However, even occasional viewing reveals that Jerry's life and identity are tied irretrievably to other characters. Virtually every episode makes evident that what Jerry does, and more importantly *who he is,* are inseparable from his social network. In *Seinfeld*, the character Jerry achieves definition through his relationships with other characters. Jerry does not tell viewers who he is. He doesn't offer us information about his character through soliloquy. Rather, viewers come to understand Jerry's identity through his associations. Though all Jerry's associations shed some light on his character, his identity is revealed most clearly through his relationships with his friends, George, Kramer, and Elaine. Viewers come to know Jerry primarily through his relations with these individuals. We learn about his insecurities through the divulgences of George. We learn about his anal-retentive streak through his exasperation with the uncontainable Kramer. We get a sense of what Jerry wants in a woman from his relationship with Elaine. We would know a different—indeed *bizarro*—Jerry, if any of these characters were to change.

Like Jerry, the identities of the other characters in *Seinfeld* are determined in and through their relations with others. We discover who George, Kramer, and Elaine are as individuals through their joint escapades and their run-ins with secondary characters such as Puddy, Mr. Pitt, and Poppie. Most viewers would attest that Elaine would not be Elaine if she wasn't browbeating George and pussyfooting around Peterman. Likewise, Kramer wouldn't be Kramer if he did not fling himself continually into Jerry's kitchen and then pilfer unapologetically from it. George would be a different George if he stopped whining to Jerry and took up with a new crew of friends. The identities of each character in *Seinfeld* are tied irrevocably to every other. We apprehend them as individuals by virtue of their relations.

Interestingly, the characters in *Seinfeld* seem to recognize that their identities are connected to others. Thus, not only do the characters' relationships with one another illustrate the fact that personal identity emerges and operates within a social framework, the characters themselves seem aware of it. Their persistent concern about what others will think reveals a certain level of recognition that their selves are mutable, socially susceptible entities. As many of us already have done, the characters in *Seinfeld* recognize that the way that they think of themselves is affected continually by what others say and do. It is this insight that motivates Jerry's concern about getting pegged for "a pick,"("The Pick") and George's anxiety that his dad might market "the Manssier"("The Doorman"). Though these could be seen as minor incidents, Jerry and George take them quite seriously. They take them seriously because both characters are aware that their selves can be sullied by the unfortunate public foray of finger into nose, or by an association with unconventional men's undergarments.

In addition to illustrating that individuals' identities are linked inescapably to others, *Seinfeld* also reveals that individuals' identities are influenced most concretely by those who are close to them. Specifically, the main characters in *Seinfeld* illustrate that friendships exert a powerful effect on an individual's sense of self. Like most sitcoms, *Seinfeld* has both main and minor characters. The main characters in *Seinfeld* are a group of close friends. Indeed, Jerry, George, Kramer, and Elaine are about as close as friends can be. Though many of the sitcom's minor characters are friendly acquaintances of the main ones, they are not friends in the way that the four main characters are. Even the intimacy that exists between the main characters and their various love interests never approximates the closeness that Jerry, George, Kramer, and Elaine have with one another.

As most viewers are aware, Jerry, George, Kramer, and Elaine are inseparable. Despite their persistent sparring with one another and their sometimes scathing sarcasm, it is obvious that these four characters care about and depend on each other. Whatever other associations and commitments Jerry, George, Kramer, and Elaine might have, it is clear that their first loyalty is to their joint friendship. Whether it means Kramer posing as Elaine's lover ("The Wallet") or George agreeing to assist Jerry with the impossible roommate switch ("The Switch"), whatever the situation, these four always come through for each other. Though typically not without comment, they put up with each other's oddities. Episode after episode reveals that they'd rather be together than with anyone else.

The friendship that exists between Jerry, George, Kramer, and Elaine binds them together in a deep and unique way. It sets them apart from other characters. Newman, for example, will forever be an outsider (a fact with which actor Wayne Knight had to reconcile himself). It causes their relationships with one another to be qualitatively different from the ones they have with other individuals. One interesting thing that the closeness between the main characters does is intensify the effect that they have on each others' identities. It makes them more influential with one another when it comes to matters of the self. In *Seinfeld*, we see repeatedly that Jerry, George, Kramer, and

Elaine are affected more by one another, than they are by other individuals. Though they are certainly concerned about and influenced greatly by what others think of them, what matters to them most is their standing with their friends. When it comes down to questions of their selves, what matters most to Jerry, George, Kramer, and Elaine are the assessments of the other members of the fabulous four.

Of course, this is not really surprising. Most of us would admit that we value the opinion of our friends more than the opinion of some stranger off the street. This is true especially when it's a question of who we think can offer the best account of our character. Unlike strangers or occasional acquaintances, we know our friends and they know us. Indeed, friends tend to know each other better than anyone else. It is my contention that friends know each other better because of the sort of relationship they have. Our friends know us so well not only because we disclose our identities more fully to them, but also because our identities are more closely linked to our friends. Though we have usually developed a sense of self by the time we enter into most of our friendships, once they are entered into these friendships affect—and typically alter—that understanding.

Like other close relationships, friendship is a relation that exerts a special influence on the self. This relation's unique capacity to affect personal identity results from the level of intimacy it encourages and the security that it offers the individuals involved. Though the effects of friendship on personal identity may not be as dramatic as the effects of the relations that individuals have with their parents or care-givers during their formative years, the friendships that individuals have in childhood and over the course of their lives do serve to shape their selves. As relational theories like Sartre's explain, a sense of self not only emerges within a social framework, it is something that is affected continually by social relations. Though our sense of self tends to achieve an increasing degree of stability as we move toward adulthood, our selves are never fixed. Rather, our selves are always evolving. As we grow and change through the course of our lives, so too does our conception of self. Our selves change subtly but constantly in response to our relations to others and the information these relations provide.

Friendships are especially influential when it comes to the self because we "let ourselves go" with our friends. Unlike in other situations in which individuals may feel that they need to be on guard or otherwise unforthcoming with respect to personal information, individuals tend to tell and show all to their friends. Individuals are less reserved in their speech and behavior with friends than they are with others generally. Individuals tend to be more open with their friends because they feel safe with them. The open and honest communications that friendships encourage are important to the formation of self because selves are formed relationally. As Sartre argues, a self is an idea that an individual forms reflexively in response to the information she derives from her social relations. Our relations with others allow us to see ourselves. In order to show us ourselves, others need information. Without ample and accurate information, others cannot do that effectively. Without a reasonable degree of openness, the understanding of self that an individual can derive from her relationships is at best a superficial one.

Real friendships however are not superficial. We trust our friends and tend to be open and honest with them. We are able derive a dependable sense of ourselves from our friendships because we share ourselves more fully with our friends and because we trust the information they offer. Our friendships contribute to the shaping of our selves because of the unique closeness and camaraderie that they promote. Unlike with other individuals, we share our deepest thoughts and dreams with our friends. The trust and closeness implicit in the relation makes it possible for us to tell our friends our most embarrassing secrets. Often without knowing what will result from the activity, we spill our hearts out to our friends. Often to our surprise, the relations we have with our friends make us to realize things we never knew about ourselves. The conversations we have with our friends commonly compel individual insight. The unexpected arguments we engage in often expose deeply held personal principles. The experiences we share disclose to us interests and dispositions that were hitherto unknown. Ultimately, giving ourselves over to friendship gives us a fuller sense of ourselves. Friendships inform our sense of self because the journey to self is one of mutual discovery. Selves are forged through our associations with others. The structures of our selves are affected by each successive relation. Friendships influence the shaping of self more than other sorts of relations because we are so deeply invested in them.

The friendship between the main characters in *Seinfeld* illustrates these facts about friendship. The relationship that exists between Jerry, George, Kramer, and Elaine demonstrates that friends have both an indelible effect on the self and a more powerful effect than other sorts of individuals. Although we can assume that Jerry, George, Kramer, and Elaine had selves prior to their friendship, it is difficult to imagine what those selves were like. Indeed, the identities of the main characters in *Seinfeld* are so interrelated, we sense that they could not remain intact in isolation. Jerry would be a different Jerry without George, Kramer, and Elaine. Each of the main characters' identities would be altered dramatically by a change in their mutual relation.

Another way that *Seinfeld* helps viewers appreciate the special influence that friends have on personal identity is by illustrating that there is qualitative difference between the friendship that the main characters have and the relationships they have with minor characters. Though minor characters certainly give viewers added insight into the individual natures of Jerry, George, Kramer, and Elaine, the removal of these characters would not alter our understanding of the main characters in a dramatic way. For example, although Elaine's various romantic relationships give viewers a fuller appreciation of her character, her identity doesn't seem to be altered profoundly by these relationships. She is not changed by these short-lived relationships in the way that she would be by a change in her relationship to Jerry. As episode after episode reveals, minor characters simply don't exert as much influence on the identities of the main characters as the main characters do on one another. Though the assessments of minor characters are often sufficient to prompt a good degree of anxiety and self-doubt, Jerry, George, Kramer, and Elaine turn unfailingly to one another when they need assurance about their selves. Others may upset their understanding of who they are, but Jerry, George, Kramer, and Elaine appeal to each other for a decisive ruling.

No Exit and *The Vault:* Sartre and *Seinfeld* on the Inescapability of Others

Ultimately, both *Seinfeld* and Sartre reveal that personal identity emerges exclusively within a social context. Both demonstrate that our relations with others are essential to the formation of self. However, *Seinfeld* serves to supplement the work of Sartre with what it tells us about friends. Though Sartre admits that selves cannot exist save in relation to others, he is not an especially cheerful advocate of relationalism. Indeed, for someone who offers a relational theory of the self he is surprisingly suspect of social relations. Though Sartre recognizes our need for others, he worries that others often exert an unhealthy influence on the formation of self. He fears that relationships often foster understandings of self that oppress rather than assist individuals in the achievement of their potential.

Sartre's play *No Exit* illustrates his suspicions of others. In *No Exit,* Sartre offers an account of three characters in hell. These characters, Garcin, Inez, and Estelle, are imprisoned together in a room. They are sentenced to stay awake and in that room with one another for eternity. Over the course of the play, it becomes obvious that none of the characters is enjoying the situation into which they have been placed. Instead, the characters all feel anxious, threatened, and oppressed by the presence of the others. They feel as if they are being judged unrelentlessly by their companions and lament that they cannot escape one another's company.

Without question, the picture that Sartre paints in *No Exit* is an unsettling one. It is perhaps more disturbing when one realizes that Sartre intends it to symbolize the human condition. According to Sartre, we are like the characters in *No Exit*. Like them, we cannot escape the fact that we are social beings. Though we might want to, we cannot get away from the fact that we need others in order to have selves. In Sartre's estimation, individuals exist in a position of uncomfortable and inescapable dependency when it comes to the consolidation of self. We can develop a sense of self only in relation to others, but all too often the assessments they offer are shallow stereotypes or demeaning characterizations that fail to recognize our intrinsic capacity for growth and change.

While Sartre's concerns are not without foundation, he seems overly suspicious of social relations. Certainly there are occasions when we feel threatened by others, violated by their gazes, and subject to their unsympathetic appraisals. Unfortunately, we do have interactions with others that have a less than positive influence on our understanding of self. However, our relationships are not all this way. *Seinfeld* shows us this. Ironically, even though the final episode of *Seinfeld* places the main characters in a situation that is surprisingly similar to the situation that Sartre describes in *No Exit,* it nonetheless succeeds in conveying a different assessment of social relations than the one offered by Sartre. In the same way that *No Exit* expresses Sartre's theory of social relations in a succinct and powerful form, the final episode of *Seinfeld* offers a concise summary of what that sitcom has to say about the effect that others have on the self.

In the spirit of *No Exit,* the last image that viewers have of Jerry, George, Kramer, and Elaine is the image of them seated together in a small prison cell. The final episode of *Seinfeld* recounts the circumstances of that imprisonment. In the last episode of the sitcom, Jerry, George, Kramer, and Elaine leave Manhattan to go on a trip. During that trip, they are arrested, put on trial, and imprisoned. The four friends are sentenced to spend a year together in jail for failing to come to the aid of an individual during an assault, thereby violating a local Good Samaritan law. The trial and imprisonment of the main characters encapsulates *Seinfeld's* message regarding both the influence of social relations on the self generally and the particular significance of friends.

During the trial depicted in the last episode of *Seinfeld,* the prosecuting attorney brings witness after witness to testify against Jerry, George, Kramer, and Elaine. Not surprisingly, the individuals brought to testify against the main characters are secondary characters who were slighted by one or more of the foursome in past episodes, individuals like the old lady Jerry mugged for a marble rye ("The Rye"). In statement after statement, these individuals offer damaging testimony about their relationships to the accused. Interestingly, in addition to helping the prosecution get a conviction, this testimony demonstrates the fact that personal identity emerges in a relational context. Specifically, insofar as the testimony refers to specific interpersonal relations and their effects, it not only illustrates how those relations have influenced the lives and identities of individual witnesses, it also reminds viewers of important events that have helped shape their conception of Jerry, George, Kramer, and Elaine. The testimony offered in *Seinfeld's* last episode reinforces the point that personal identity cannot be separated from social relations.

Another thing that the final episode of *Seinfeld* does is reiterate how important friends are to the development of self. Although virtually every episode of the sitcom speaks to the significance of friends, the events and images of the last episode are particularly effective in the way they draw our attention to the unique role that friends play in identity formation. In the last episode, two elements serve to confirm the point that friends exert a special influence on the self. They are the events of the trial and the closing image of the foursome in prison.

The trial reinforces the notion that friends are of unique significance to the self through the testimony it offers. Although the bulk of the testimony is from secondary characters, Jerry, George, Kramer, and Elaine also testify on their own behalf. What is telling about the two sorts of testimony are the different impressions they serve to evoke. Though the testimony of secondary characters convinces the judge and jury that Jerry, George, Kramer and Elaine are insufferable individuals, it doesn't convince viewers. It doesn't convince viewers because viewers have a more intimate understanding of Jerry, George, Kramer, and Elaine. Unlike secondary characters who know Jerry, George, Kramer, and Elaine from the outside—perhaps even from one incident—viewers know the foursome from the inside. We know the depth of their friendship and how they relate to one another. We know that while Jerry, George, Kramer, and Elaine have certainly done bad things, they aren't bad people. Although the testimony offered by secondary characters does say something about Jerry's, George's, Kramer's, and Elaine's characters, viewers know that it doesn't tell the whole story. The trial testimony demonstrates that in order to understand the main characters' identities completely, one needs to consider their friends.

Last but not least, the closing image of the final episode of *Seinfeld* illustrates the special relevance of friends to personal identity. Perhaps more powerfully than anything else, the image of Jerry, George, Kramer, and Elaine in prison solidifies our understanding that friends have an inalterable and inescapable effect on our selves. Where Sartre's message in *No Exit* is that we cannot escape the impact that others in general have on the formation of self, *Seinfeld*'s message is more precise. By imprisoning close friends, not complete strangers, *Seinfeld* conveys the point that friends exert a more powerful influence on personal identity than other individuals. The closing image of *Seinfeld* reveals that of all the others who inform personal identity the ones we really cannot escape are our friends. Where the animosity of the scene in *No Exit* suggests that our dependency on others is oppressive, the friendly chatter emanating from the foursome's cell in the last episode of Seinfeld suggests that our reliance on others might not be so bad.

In conclusion, both Sartre and *Seinfeld* reveal that others are essential to the development of self. Both Sartre and *Seinfeld* demonstrate that we discover our identities with others. They reveal that subjectivity is predicated on sociality. What *Seinfeld* does more effectively than Sartre is illustrate the positive role that friends play in the development of personal identity. The sitcom reveals that our friendships affect our selves more deeply than do other sorts of relations. It illustrates that friendship facilitates self-discovery. Instead of fostering apprehension about friendship, *Seinfeld* evokes an appreciation of the security that this relation provides. *Seinfeld* shows how much we depend on our friends for our identity. It makes us appreciate how much we need our friends to be ourselves.

8

Wittgenstein and *Seinfeld* on the Commonplace

KELLY DEAN JOLLEY

Where does our investigation get its importance from, since it seems only to destroy everything interesting, that is, all that is great and important? (As it were all the buildings, leaving behind only bits of stone and rubble.) What we are destroying is nothing but houses of cards and we are clearing up the ground of language on which they stand.

—Wittgenstein, *Philosophical Investigations* 118[1]

Philosophical Investigations

Anyone familiar with Ludwig Wittgenstein's *Philosophical Investigations* and also with *Seinfeld* is likely to be struck by their similar, contrapuntal structure.

Wittgenstein characterizes *Philosophical Investigations* as "really only an album,"[2] containing a number of philosophical remarks that are "sketches of landscapes . . . made in the course

---

[1] The number 118 refers to a section rather than a page. This applies to all references here to Wittgenstein's *Philosophical Investigations*.

[2] Wittgenstein, Ludwig. *Philosophical Investigations,* tr. G.E.M. Anscombe (New York: Macmillan, 1958), p. ix. All quotations in this section are from the Preface (ix–x). All other quotations from *Philosophical Investigations* will be accompanied by the number of the remark quoted.

of . . . long and involved journeyings." Some have taken Wittgenstein to be confessing failure by characterizing the book in these ways. Indeed, he seems to invite this way of taking his characterizations when he admits that he pictured the book initially as a series of thoughts that "should proceed from one subject to another in a natural order and without breaks." He continues to say that he eventually realized that he would not succeed in writing the book he pictured:

> After several unsuccessful attempts to weld my results together into such a whole, I realized that I should never succeed. The best that I could write would never be more than philosophical remarks; my thoughts were soon crippled if I tried to force them on in any single direction against their natural inclination. —And this was, of course, connected with the very nature of the investigation.

Although Wittgenstein may sound as if he is confessing failure, his last comment suggests that he is not doing so. His last comment rates his "failure" as necessary. His initial picture of his book is an illusion—an illusion about the very nature of the investigation he is conducting. Wittgenstein's sort of philosophical investigation cannot proceed in a single direction, without breaks.

What sort of philosophical investigation "compels us to travel over a wide field of thought criss-cross in every direction"? What sort requires sketches of landscapes? What sort requires an album? To answer these questions it will help to take a look at some of the landscape sketches in the album. Before we do that, however, allow me to provide some preliminary remarks on *Seinfeld.*

Seinfeld

In "The Pilot"—the episode in which Jerry and George pilot the *Jerry* show—Jerry remarks that *Jerry* is "a show about nothing." Jerry's remark is clearly meant to characterize *Seinfeld* as well. Like Wittgenstein's characterizing of *Philosophical Investigations,* Jerry's double-faced characterizing of *Jerry* and *Seinfeld* can seem to confess failure. However, even though *Jerry* is dropped by the network president mere minutes after the pilot airs, *Jerry* is not a failure. Virtually every character from earlier episodes of *Seinfeld* is shown watching *Jerry*; and, Jerry, George, and Elaine are all extremely happy with the pilot. And *Seinfeld* itself is, of course, no failure.

The show is a show about nothing, but this does not make it a failure. The "failure" is necessary; and, what Jerry characterizes as nothing is only nothing relative to an illusion about what a show must be (about). The sort of show *Seinfeld* is requires that it flirt with not being a show (since a show about nothing and no show are hard to tell apart).

But what sort of show can be "a show about nothing"? What sort of show is a show without a plot, without a central romantic couple, without even one completely likable character? The answer to these questions is connected to the very nature of the show.

Philosophical Investigations, Again

In *Philosophical Investigations* 129, Wittgenstein confides to his reader that

> The aspects of things that are most important for us are hidden because of their simplicity and familiarity. (One is unable to notice something—because it is always before one's eyes.) The real foundations of his enquiry do not strike a man at all. Unless *that* fact has at some time struck him. —And this means: we fail to see what, once seen, is most striking and powerful.

And, in 596, he comments on

> The feeling of 'familiarity' and of 'naturalness'. It is easier to get at a feeling of unfamiliarity and unnaturalness. Or, at *feelings*. For not everything which is unfamiliar to us makes an impression of unfamiliarity upon us. Here one has to consider what we call "unfamiliar". If a boulder lies on the road, we know it for a boulder, but perhaps not for the one which has always lain there. We recognize a man, say, as a man, but not as an acquaintance. There are feelings of old acquaintance: they are sometimes expressed by a particular way of looking or by the words: "The same old room!" (which I occupied many years before and now returning find unchanged). Equally there are feelings of strangeness. I stop short, look at the object or man questioningly or mistrustfully, say "I find it all strange."—But the existence of this feeling of strangeness does

not give us a reason for saying that every object which we know well and which does not seem strange to us gives us a feeling of familiarity.—We think that, as it were, the place once filled by the feeling of strangeness must surely be occupied *somehow*. The place for this kind of atmosphere is there, and if one of them is not in possession of it, then another is.

Wittgenstein is pointing out that although there are feelings of familiarity and of unfamiliarity, not everything which is familiar to us causes a feeling of familiarity and not everything which is unfamiliar to us causes a feeling of unfamiliarity. This may seem obvious enough, but Wittgenstein points it out because he believes that pressures we are under when we philosophize make it easy to miss. In the remarks preceding 596, Wittgenstein is attacking the illusion that meaning is a mental activity—in particular, that meaning a sentence is a mental act. (This is the illusion Wittgenstein attacks over and over again in *Philosophical Investigations*. In remarks 1 and 2 he is already attacking "the philosophical concept of meaning"; in 693, the last remark in Part 1, his Parthian shot is "And nothing is more wrong-headed than calling meaning a mental activity! Unless, that is, one is setting out to produce confusion.") Wittgenstein is trying to show that saying and meaning a sentence is not a matter of saying a sentence accompanied by a feeling of familiarity. The fact that a speaker's saying of a sentence is accompanied by a feeling of familiarity does not make it the case that the speaker means the sentence he says. Moreover, the fact that a speaker's saying of a sentence is not accompanied by a feeling of familiarity does not make it the case that the speaker does not mean the sentence he says. An accompanying feeling of familiarity neither is the speaker's meaning the sentence, nor is it the mark of his meaning the sentence. Typically, when a speaker says a sentence and means it, there is no accompanying feeling of familiarity; indeed, there is typically no accompanying feeling at all.

Why, then, would anyone insist that a feeling of familiarity accompanies any sentence that a speaker says and means? This is where 596 enters the discussion. Typically, when a speaker says a sentence and does not mean it, there is an accompanying feeling of unfamiliarity (or, unnaturalness). For example, if a speaker of English is asked to say the sentence

I said that that 'that' that that man used was used correctly
in surroundings in which no one man has said 'that', the saying

of the sentence will typically be accompanied by a feeling of unfamiliarity. (The feeling will typically accompany the saying of a sentence even much more common than the example I have given, so long as the surroundings in which the sentence is said are suitably inappropriate.) The fact that typically a sentence that a speaker says and does not mean is accompanied by a feeling of unfamiliarity then begins to exert philosophical pressure. The fact makes it seem necessary that the place occupied by a feeling of unfamiliarity when a speaker says a sentence and does not mean it must be occupied by a feeling of familiarity when he says a sentence and does mean it. The sentence, we might say, cannot go out alone: it must take either the feeling of familiarity or unfamiliarity along for company.

596 exerts philosophical counter-pressure. Wittgenstein reminds his reader that the absence of a feeling of unfamiliarity does not require the presence of a feeling of familiarity. A speaker can say and mean a sentence without any feeling at all; a speaker can say and not mean a sentence without any feeling at all. *Feelings* are easier to get at than meanings. But that does not make them meanings or make them marks of meanings. The philosophical pressure exerted by the typical accompaniment of sentences that are said and not meant by feelings of unfamiliarity makes us hypostasize feelings of familiarity where typically there are none (cf. 598). But the philosophical pressure can—and should—be resisted. 596 shows us how—and why.

I realize that discussing 596 at length may seem bootless. It is not. Discussing it at length accomplishes two things: (1) It makes clear the target of Wittgenstein's attacks in *Philosophical Investigations,* the philosophical concept of meaning. And, it makes clear Wittgenstein's central type of attack on the target: Wittgenstein will everywhere confront our apparent need for a philosophical concept of meaning with commonplaces, superficies. (2) Understanding 129 demands that we come to terms with Wittgenstein's handling of familiarity. Consider: In 129 Wittgenstein claims that the things most important for his sort of philosophical investigation are hidden. They are hidden by their familiarity. How can this be? 596 provides an important part of the answer: Not everything that is familiar causes a feeling of familiarity. Our feelings are not a reliable guide to what is familiar. If they were, then it would be hard to see how something familiar could be hidden: our attention would be drawn to it because of the feeling it caused. Since what is familiar need not cause a feeling of familiarity, the familiar often confronts us unacknowledged, like the boulder we recognize as a boulder, but not as the same old boulder.

Familiarity hides the aspects of things of the most importance to Wittgenstein's philosophical investigations. The real foundations of Wittgenstein's philosophical investigations go unnoticed because they are omnipresent. Wittgenstein claims that the real foundations are not striking until the fact that they are not striking becomes striking. How, though, is *that* supposed to happen? Here, at last, we are in the vicinity of the answers to our earlier questions about Wittgenstein's philosophical investigations.

If the aspects of things of the most importance to Wittgenstein's philosophical investigations are not striking, then no list of them will be striking. Wittgenstein cannot simply list the real foundations because the list would seem a list of the most common of commonplaces—a list of things beneath notice. There would be no way to make someone accept the claim that the listed commonplaces are the real foundations of philosophical investigation. (After all, philosophical investigation is supposed to be oriented away from commonplaces, oriented toward uncommonplaces.) To get the commonplaces acknowledged as the real foundations of philosophical investigation, Wittgenstein is forced into writing an album, into sketching landscapes. Since listing the real foundations in a natural order and without breaks would fail to get the real foundations noticed, Wittgenstein does—and has to do—something different. He makes *remarks*: he nags, he describes, he re-arranges, he reminds. He does this in order to reorient philosophical investigation, to bring his reader to see the commonplaces doing their real foundational work.

So it is Wittgenstein's commitment to drawing attention to commonplaces that requires an album, that requires sketches of landscapes. Wittgenstein's sort of philosophical investigation is an investigation, not into profundities, but rather into superficies. Superficies do the real work in philosophy; they are the means to dispelling philosophical illusions (think of Wittgenstein's attack on the philosophical concept of meaning), but they are what philosophers look through and not what they see.

Seinfeld, Again

I hope that discussing *Philosophical Investigations* will make discussing *Seinfeld* easier. Wittgenstein's commitment to the commonplaces, his investigation of superficies, is mirrored in *Seinfeld's* commitment to the commonplaces of contemporary life, its investigation of the superficies of contemporary life. *Seinfeld* is a show about nothing—because it is a show about what goes unnoticed because of its familiarity. The show reorients its audience to the real foundations of contemporary life.

The way *Seinfeld* reorients its audience is closely related to the way that *Philosophical Investigations* gets its reader to see commonplaces. *Philosophical Investigations* takes the form of an album—a series of remarks—as opposed to the normal philosophical form, the finished essay. *Seinfeld* takes the form of an album—a series of vignettes—as opposed to the normal sitcom form, the developed plot. What *Seinfeld* is trying to get its audience to see is something that a developed plot would only obscure. A plot, naturally enough, orients the audience's attention to itself. By doing so, the plot obscures commonplaces, since they are at most the means by which the plot is developed. By rejecting the developed plot, *Seinfeld* reorients the audience's attention to the commonplaces.

Seinfeld, again like *Philosophical Investigations,* also shows itself aware of how difficult it is to keep attention oriented to commonplaces. In *Philosophical Investigations,* Wittgenstein nags, describes, re-arranges and reminds. *Seinfeld* resorts to many of the same tactics: the particular commonplaces to which an episode orients attention recur in each, or in most, of the episodes' vignettes. Each time they recur, the commonplaces are in a different setting, or are slightly transposed, or are differently reacted to by the characters. *Seinfeld* nags by insisting that the commonplaces recur, that the commonplaces are mentioned repeatedly by the characters or are ignored repeatedly by the characters.

Musicalizing the Commonplace

I began with a tease: an all-too-brief comment about the similar, contrapuntal structures of *Philosophical Investigations* and *Seinfeld.* I want to recur to my tease. In Aldous Huxley's novel about contrapuntal structures, *Point Counter Point,* one of the characters, Philip Quarles, writes in his notebook:

> The musicalization of fiction . . . Meditate on Beethoven . . . The changes of moods, the abrupt transitions . . . More interesting still, the modulations, not merely from one key to another, but from mood to mood. A theme is stated, then developed, pushed out of shape, imperceptibly deformed, until, though still recognizably the same, it has become quite different. In sets of variations the process is carried a step further. Those incredible Diabelli variations, for example. The whole range of thought and feeling, yet all in organic relation to a ridiculous little waltz tune. Get this into a novel. How?[3]

I have been trying to shed light on how *Philosophical Investigations* and *Seinfeld* get *this* into a book of philosophy and into a sitcom. Wittgenstein musicalizes the commonplace for philosophy; *Seinfeld* musicalizes it for the sitcom. For each, the commonplaces are reliably revealed only when the reader or the audience recognizes organic relations—of remark to remark, or of vignette to vignette. That in *Philosophical Investigations* remark stands in organic relation to remark, or in *Seinfeld,* vignette to vignette, demonstrates the real foundational work done by the commonplaces. The commonplaces in organic relations organize our lives: the *commonplaces are the tune of our lives.* But the tune of the commonplaces, like the music of the spheres, is hard to hear—because we hear it all the time. Both *Philosophical Investigations* and *Seinfeld* strive to teach "a new way of hearkening, some kind of receptivity" (232). For both, it is not ignorance (the state), but rather ignoring (the activity) that needs combating. It is not something we do not know which is the problem, but rather something we will not do.

Finale

The bathos of *Philosophical Investigations* gathers most affectingly in 118, the remark that I quoted as my epigraph. Wittgenstein admits to himself that his investigation is unimpor-

---

[3] Huxley, Aldous. *Point Counter Point* (Garden City, NY: Doubleday, Doran, and Company, 1928), pp. 293–94.

tant, at least in the sense that it builds nothing, creates nothing great or important. But, in that sense, Wittgenstein thinks all philosophical investigation is unimportant. Philosophy builds nothing, creates nothing, except houses of cards. To think that philosophy has built well and surely, that it has created things of greatness and importance, is to suffer from an illusion—the same sort of illusion that makes the finished essay seem the only form for philosophy, or that makes the philosophical conception of meaning seem fated. Wittgenstein attacks philosophy's houses of cards, pulls them down. He does so because our illusional fascination with the houses of cards blinds us to the commonplaces that support them, the ground of language.

The bathos of *Seinfeld* gathers in Jerry's comment about *Jerry:* "It's a show about nothing!" Jerry admits to himself that *Jerry*—and to his audience that *Seinfeld*—is unimportant, at least in the sense that no plot is developed. The lesson of *Seinfeld* is that our illusional fascination with the developed plot blinds us to the commonplaces that develop the plot, the ground of contemporary life.

Philosophical Investigations and *Seinfeld* each cultivate freedom from a certain illusion. To do this, each becomes a pseudomorph of the source of the illusion from which it frees: *Philosophical Investigations* is a pseudomorph of the finished essay; *Seinfeld* of the developed plot. To free a person from an illusion, it is necessary for the freeing device to enter into the space of illusion—that is, it is necessary for the freeing device to resemble what illudes so that the illuded person pays heed to the freeing device, to the pseudomorph. The trick is then to deform the pseudomorph—to deform it so as to reveal that *the illusion itself* (and not merely the pseudomorph) is optional. In this way, the hardness of the illuded 'must' is softened; what is overlook may then be seen. And only what is seen can be seen as striking or powerful, or great or important.[4]

---

[4] I thank Jody Graham, Alice Crary, and Paul Muench for helpful comments and discussions.

Untimely Meditations by the Water Cooler

9

The Costanza Maneuver: Is it Rational for George to "Do the Opposite"?

JASON HOLT

D'you ever notice how people think they top you in an argument just by saying, "You're being irrational"? It never works. The other person just gets mad, which kind of proves you right before the fact. But you still don't win the argument.

No one wants to be called irrational. Deep down, even those who espouse misology (hatred of reason, not to be confused with misogyny) flinch at the very threat of it, from the Gen-X flake to the New-Age sponge. Reason is one of the things we pride ourselves on as a species, but that pride is often inflated, a fact exploited to great effect by *Seinfeld*. In the character of George especially, we see writ large the symptoms and causes of an impoverished reason. Being rational is an important part of being human—our lives depend on it—yet it can be funny to see just how far short of the ideal we can fall. Since Basil Fawlty, perhaps no character has better illustrated this than George Costanza.

Of all the *Seinfeld* episodes, one of the most memorable pits George against the forces constantly at work to defeat him—his own impulses. One day, in conversation with Jerry, he reports a revelation:

GEORGE: It all became very clear to me . . . that every decision I've ever made, in my entire life, has been wrong. My life is the complete opposite of everything I want it to be. Every instinct I have, in every aspect of life, be it something to wear, something to eat . . . it's all been wrong.[1]

As George sees it, whether he acts on decision or impulse, his behavior is always "wrong." His actions fail to bring about and, more than this, often *preclude* the desired results. As anyone familiar with *Seinfeld* knows, George is not just ineffectual in achieving his ends, he is self-defeating. Whatever causes him to act as he does, his attempts at victory seal his defeat, and bring about the very opposite of what he wants. In a rare moment of clarity, George discovers something we have laughed at all along—that he is his own worst enemy.

Most of us, when struck by an epiphany, act accordingly. Perhaps we put the insight to good use, improving our lot, our ways of thinking, even our character. At least we let it sink in. We mull it over, and appreciate its significance. What does George do? He has lunch. Lucky for him, though, a residuum of his insight remains:

WAITRESS: Tuna on toast, coleslaw, cup of coffee.

GEORGE: Yeah. No, no, no, wait a minute. I always have tuna on toast. Nothing's ever worked out for me with tuna on toast. I want the complete opposite of tuna on toast. Chicken salad, on rye, untoasted, with a side of potato salad—and a cup of tea.

Much as changing his order to the "opposite" is an act of hopeless futility, or hapless irony, it gets the ball rolling toward what will become, at least in this episode, George's guiding principle.

Here is how it happens. Elaine notices an attractive woman looking at George. She reports this, and tells him to approach the woman. He is loath to do so, but where Elaine plants the seed, Jerry adds fertilizer:

---

[1] All *Seinfeld* quotations in this essay are from the episode "The Opposite."

JERRY: Well, here's your chance to try the opposite. Instead of tuna salad and being intimidated by women, chicken salad and going right up to them.

GEORGE: Yeah, I should do the opposite, I should.

JERRY: If every instinct you have is wrong, then the opposite would have to be right.

GEORGE: Yes, I will do the opposite. I used to sit here and do nothing, and regret it for the rest of the day. So now I will do the opposite, and I will do something.

Of course Jerry's motivation here is to amuse himself, as always. George knows this, but makes his approach nonetheless.

It is not altogether clear why George approaches the woman. Perhaps he does so for the sake of self-mockery, or out of a tragic sense of life—he might as well contribute to the joke at his expense (Absurdist George). Perhaps too it is out of a genuine desire to test Jerry's hypothesis, made in jest but potentially useful (Curious George). Being George however, it is likely more the former that moves him to action:

GEORGE: My name is 'George'. I'm unemployed and I live with my parents.

VICTORIA: I'm Victoria. Hi.

Doing the opposite wins Victoria's interest. Repeated efforts sustain it. Later, in an interview with the New York Yankees, George meets team-owner Steinbrenner (another George), and the strategy really pays off:

GEORGE S: Nice to meet you.

GEORGE C: Well, I wish I could say the same. But I must say, with all due respect, I find it very hard to see the logic behind some of the moves you've made with this fine organization. In the past twenty years, you have caused myself, and the city of New York, a good deal of distress, as we've watched you take our beloved Yankees and reduce them to a laughing-stock, all for the glorification of your *massive* ego!

GEORGE S: Hire this man!

After his success with (the aptly named) Victoria, and before his success with the Yankees, George adopts the strategy of doing the opposite—what I'll call the *Costanza Maneuver*—as a principle of action. Witness how George's tentative approach to Victoria blossoms to full-blown confidence in the job-interview.

Leaving the episode aside for the moment, we can ask whether it is *rational* for George to do the opposite, a question of some philosophical interest, and which naturally comes to mind when the laughter dies down. Answering this question is my chief concern in this essay, and will require touching on a variety of topics apropos of *Seinfeld* and philosophy, including not only reason and rationality, but morality and virtue ethics, decision-theory, human nature, and—as a special case-study for psychology—George's mind.

Reason and Right

The first thing to be clear on is what exactly the Costanza Maneuver is. What does it mean to "do the opposite"? For George, doing the opposite means doing the opposite of what he would normally do. Whatever inclinations he has, be they the product of impulse or deliberation, the Costanza Maneuver inverts them, and bids him do the opposite. What this amounts to in many cases is far from obvious, a significant problem to be discussed in due course.

One thing to notice about the Costanza Maneuver is that by its own lights it has to admit of exceptions. Were George to apply it consistently, he would never be able to act at all, much less in accordance with the principle, except to keep applying the principle *ad infinitum*. If the Costanza Maneuver is taken to oppose *all* inclinations, then it rules out not only those that George wants opposed, but also those the principle recommends—inclinations to do the opposite. Opposing these inclinations would bring George back to square one, since an opposite's opposite is simply what you started with. Worse yet, George would have to apply the principle over and over again, without end, in a pointless regression barely more absurd than his own life. Like something out of Beckett, no?

Happily this is not much of a problem, for the Costanza Maneuver is intended to apply only to George's natural, basic inclinations, and not to those the principle recommends. So long as we limit the scope of application in this way, there does not appear to be any logical difficulty in applying the principle. So conceived, the principle is at least coherent, and thus a candidate for being rational. When I speak of George's inclinations, then, I mean those that are basic and natural to him, opposable by the Costanza Maneuver.

Earlier I said that the Costanza Maneuver is an action-guiding principle. Now most people, when they think of guiding principles, have moral principles in mind—words to live by, secular or sacred in origin. It is important to realize that the Costanza Maneuver is not a moral principle. All moral principles may be action-guiding, but not all action-guiding principles are moral. This does not mean the Costanza Maneuver is immoral, but rather that it is amoral, lying outside the moral sphere. Questions about whether it is good, or morally right, to pull the Costanza Maneuver are beside the point of whether it is rational to do so.

Many philosophers, some still living, some long dead, resist the distinction I am drawing between rationality and morality. For various reasons, they find appealing, and go to great lengths to justify, the notion that intellectual and moral virtues converge, that reason and right are one and the same. Without going into too much detail, arguments to this effect are notoriously hard to defend. The idea of a perfectly rational bad guy is just too plausible, as is that of the good-natured simpleton. Illustrations abound. Look at the more formulaic movies coming out of Hollywood. It seems that reason and right just *have* to diverge somewhere. Morality tells you what to do irrespective of your desires. Reason tells you what to do to achieve your desires, whatever they may be. This leaves open the distinct possibility that, in certain cases, doing the right thing means sacrificing one's own interests. That is why being moral seems to go hand in hand with self-sacrifice. Moral people—think of your own examples—at some point give of themselves. It may be rational to give of oneself for some further desired end, or in the name of some cause, but although it can be rational to be moral, it need not be. One can be rational without giving a second thought to moral concerns, much less making a first effort at being moral. This can happen when the desired ends are either evil, incompatible with the good, or simply in areas where morality does not apply.

My discussion of morality is by way of showing what the
Costanza Maneuver is *not*. It purports to be not a moral principle but a rational one.[2] None of the *Seinfeld* characters is particularly moral, perhaps Kramer, but certainly not George.[3] Yet
the latter's namesake strategy may indeed be rational. Now that
we know what the strategy is not, we can move on to what it
is, and discuss in more detail what it means to be rational.

Three Kinds of Rationality

What does it mean to be rational? The answer is somewhat subtle and complex, in part because there are various senses of 'reason' and 'rational', different ways these words are used. When
we call someone irrational we may mean a number of things.
We may mean they hold unjustified opinions, that they miss the
point, or have turned a blind eye to certain things, denied the
obvious, and so on. We may mean that they act crazy, or contrary to their better judgment—that they should have known
better. Or we may mean that what they are after is silly, not
worthwhile, too far removed from what they really want, or
what they should want to achieve further ends. One can be
rational or irrational in what one *thinks,* in what one *does,* and
arguably in what one *wants.*

Consider some examples. It is rational to think that one
should carry an umbrella in the rain to avoid getting wet, but
irrational to think that leaving the oven on at home will achieve
the same end. Likewise it is rational to go to the corner store if
one is out of milk, irrational to pray that a fresh carton will mate-
rialize in the fridge on its own. It is rational to want to be happy,
irrational to want the Washington Senators to win the next World
Series—as a matter of common knowledge, the Senators no
longer exist. There simply is no such team, and so it makes no
sense to root for them.

Talking about rational and irrational desires is somewhat
problematic because many wants are not subject to evaluation
or informed change. Occasionally I like social-tea biscuits with

---

[2] For a different position on this see Aeon J. Skoble, "Virtue Ethics in TV's
Seinfeld," in this volume.
[3] For a different position on this see Robert Epperson, "*Seinfeld* and the Moral
Life," in this volume.

my coffee, but is this the sort of thing I could ever justify? The desire to have the occasional social-tea seems purely a matter of taste, non-negotiable in a rational forum. Still, some desires do seem patently silly, like the desire to have everyone wear paper hats on the stroke of midnight next January 23rd. That's just bonkos. So while some desires are not terribly rational or irrational, some seem irrational, while still others seem rational. Consider the desire to protect one's family from harm.

Questions about the rational status of desire are not really important here, since we can assume that there is nothing wrong with what George wants. The course of *Seinfeld* supports this assumption; what is so amusing about George is less what he wants and more the way he goes about trying to get it. What does he want? Success, as do we all. He wants to win the game of life, to be liked, to impress potential sex-partners, to succeed in business without really trying. If desires are evaluable in this way at all, what George wants is not irrational. So in examining whether it is rational for George to do the opposite, we have to look not at his desires, but at his behavior, and the thought-processes (or lack thereof) behind it. To help get clear on what exactly we mean when we ask whether it is rational for George to do the opposite, it would be helpful to distinguish three different kinds of rationality. Within philosophy itself there are various such concepts, and it is all too easy to confuse one for the other.

First, notice that actions can often be *rationalized* by beliefs and desires, even if the beliefs are patently irrational. Normally we say that someone is rationalizing when they make excuses for their behavior, coming up with them on the spot, in an attempt to avoid responsibility, an attempt that is usually obvious and therefore unsuccessful. In a philosophical sense, however, beliefs and desires rationalize behavior when they make sense of it, regardless of whether the beliefs themselves are justified. We can make sense of a man's juggling at a party if we know he wants to impress women and believes that by his juggling he will impress them. Why is he juggling? *Because* he wants to impress women.

Practically all behavior is rational in this way. Citing the right belief/desire pair makes sense of people's behavior. But this is a very weak sense in which an action may be rational—what we might call *minimal* rationality, a reflection of the fact that we have to presuppose a minimal sort of reason to even understand what someone says or does. Both in general and in pulling the Costanza Maneuver, George is rational in that we can easily understand his behavior. Why does he do the opposite? Because he believes it will get him what he wants. Notice that George's behavior here would be minimally rational whether or not he got what he wanted. Were the Costanza Maneuver to fail, we would still know what George was trying to accomplish by pulling it.

At the other extreme we have a different, and much stronger, sense of being rational—what we might call *maximal* rationality. This is the region inhabited by the few, the supremely talented: Mr. Spock, Sherlock Holmes, Socrates. These are the icons of intellect, beings with ideal faculties of reason. They are not just reasonable, but rational as can be. They are expert problem-solvers, performing feats of computation and inference well beyond the normal thinker's ken. They act efficiently, without hesitation, cutting to the heart of the matter, maximizing the achievement of maximal ends. Under the best conditions, almost no one can even approximate the achievements of such well-oiled thinking-machines.

Clearly, what we are after is a notion of rationality somewhere in between the minimal and the maximal—what we might call *medial* rationality, reason with a human face, intelligent, but human. Let us zero in on the target by considering more explicitly the relationship between means (actions) and ends (desired results). Most actions presuppose a goal; one does things to bring about certain results. We already concede that what George desires is okay, even though there may be more worthwhile things for him to strive for. What we want to know is whether the Costanza Maneuver, and specifically George's adoption of it as an action-guiding principle, is appropriately related to his desired ends.

You do not have to be a genius to be medially rational, you do not have to be a great problem-solver, and you do not have to perform extraordinary feats of computation or inference. Nor do you have to act most efficiently, without question or pause, or maximize the achievement of maximal ends. You can be emotional, even impulsive. But you have to be pretty good at discovering and doing what to do to get what you want—you have to have passable instrumental reason. An action-guiding principle like the Costanza Maneuver does not have to be the best of all possible strategies, it just has to be a good one. And for it to be a good one, you have to know two things: first, that it has a good chance of getting you what you want; and second, that you can implement it in a quorum of applicable cases.

Now we have a litmus test for finding out whether it is rational for George to do the opposite. The Costanza Maneuver is (medially) rational for George to adopt if (and only if) George has good reason to think it both reliable and feasible. If both conditions hold, then it is rational for George to do the opposite. But if either fails, it is not rational. I will argue that neither condition holds, and that therefore it is irrational for George to do the opposite. Not only is the Costanza Maneuver neither reliable nor feasible as a matter of fact, George lacks sufficient reason to suppose otherwise.

Getting What You Want

I want to argue that the Costanza Maneuver is an unreliable means of getting George what he wants, and that he has no good reason to think otherwise. But am I not missing the point? The Costanza Maneuver works for George, and surely that is what counts. Perhaps I ask too much. Granted, in his efforts to do the opposite, George gets what he wants. He wins and sustains Victoria's interest. He secures a job with the Yankees, along with several more minor victories, all in the space of a single episode. Besides which, since George does the opposite of what he would normally do, and since what he would normally do is irrational, it seems he must be rational to do the opposite.

But the opposite of something irrational is not necessarily rational. An example: It is unwise to sink your life-savings into a high-risk investment, because the odds are just too good you will lose your shirt. The opposite would seem to be sticking with low-yield but secure ventures, or not investing at all. But if you need investment income, the rational move may not be to avoid risky ventures altogether, but to invest part of your savings in them. That is, it may be irrational to do either one thing or the opposite, the rational course being somewhere in the middle. Another example: If you are cold and in the vicinity of a fire, it is rational neither to stay away nor throw yourself on the flames. These would seem to be opposites, yet both are irrational. Acting in opposition to irrational impulses does not by itself guarantee rationality.

Merely getting what you want is no benchmark of reason. Likewise, being rational is no benchmark of getting what you want, because even if one is maximally rational, there are always other elements in the picture, circumstances beyond one's knowledge or control. Although following the course of reason is no guarantee of success, rational decisions certainly facilitate the achievement of desired ends. I bring this up to suggest not that successful means can be irrational, but that being successful and being rational are two different things.

Why? The answer is that success can be and often is a matter of luck, *dumb* luck. Imagine you are playing draw poker, and the hand you are dealt yields two salient options. You can discard one and go for the outside straight, or you can discard two and go for the flush. Although a flush beats a straight, the odds are such that—as a general rule—it is irrational to go for the flush. If you go for the flush, you may get it. And if you get it, the chances are good you will win. But the chances of drawing a straight *and* winning are much better than the chances of drawing a flush and winning. If you go for the low-percentage move, and it pays off, that does not mean you were rational to do so.

Take lotteries for example, which yield about $1 for every $5 spent. If you win the lottery, that does not mean that buying the ticket was rational. It was irrational if you were in it solely for the money, although many people get a harmless thrill in the bargain. The minimal expense is often more than outweighed by anticipatory pleasure, in which case there is nothing irrational about it. Notice that George's pleasure derives not from any such anticipation, but rather and solely from his astounding success. Thus George's doing the opposite cannot be rational in the same way buying lottery tickets can.

By now it should be clear that mere success is no measure of reason. The (achievement of) ends do(es) not (rationally) justify the means. Despite George's success, then, we must ask whether the Costanza Maneuver is reliable and, more importantly, whether George is right to bet on its being so.

What are the Odds?

Is the Costanza Maneuver a reliable strategy? Will it *tend* to get George what he wants, or does he just happen to luck out? On the surface it certainly seems reliable. From ordering chicken salad near the beginning, to telling his parents he loves them near the end, George does the opposite no less than ten times. In a few cases it is not clear whether the strategy is of any value. But in most cases the attempt is a very palpable success. As I score it, George's batting average is around .800, which certainly seems reliable enough.

Consider, however, that although a strategy may work 80 percent of the time in a certain range of cases, this may amount to nothing more than what gamblers call a lucky streak. Note the trivial fact that the Costanza Maneuver works in the episode because the writers wrote it that way. And they wrote it that way because it is funny, realistic or not. Admittedly, part of the strength of *Seinfeld* lies in a ruthless sense of realism, even in finding absurdity in the mundane, and vice versa. But we should be wary of drawing any real conclusions from the plot of a sit-com, even a top-shelf sit-com like *Seinfeld*. One gets the sense that the Costanza Maneuver works for George not because it is a good strategy, but because it would be absurd, the dumbest possible luck, for it ever to work.

If we look at George's individual at-bats, rather than his batting average, it becomes clear just how unlikely his successes are. When Elaine first pressures him to approach Victoria, he is right to retort:

> GEORGE: Elaine, bald men, with no jobs, and no money, who live with their parents, don't approach strange women.

Why not? Because they know that by and large they will incur from beautiful women not interest but wrath. Later, George goes ballistic at some annoying, vaguely thuggish movie-goers:

> GEORGE: Shut your traps and stop kicking the seats! We're trying to watch the movie! And if I have to tell you again, we're gonna take it outside, and I'm gonna show you what it's like. You understand me? Now shut your mouths,

or I'll shut them for you. And if you think I'm kidding, just
try me. Try me. Because I would love it!

How likely is it that such a rant would quiet *thuggish* movie-
goers? Not bloody likely. What are the odds of getting a job by
being rude to the boss? Slim indeed.

Now does George have any reason to think otherwise? His
initial efforts at the opposite do bear a superficial resemblance
to hypothesis-testing. Further efforts are spurred on by initial
successes, which appear to confirm the hypothesis. Seems rational enough. But come on. George's success is not just a matter
of luck, it is obviously so. The hypothesis is only spuriously confirmed, and we know this. George, too, should know better, and
on some level I think he does:

> GEORGE: This has been the dream of my life ever since I was
> a child. And it's all happening because I'm completely
> ignoring every urge toward common sense and good
> judgment I've ever had.

George's primary pleasure comes from success, but there is
also—look for it—the more ironic pleasure of knowing he does
not, in any sense, deserve it. That is part of the reason his success is so funny, precisely because it is based on a strategy that
we all know is unreliable—George included. It shouldn't work,
but does. There's the rub.

Long-Term Feasibility

Doing the opposite is not a reliable strategy, nor does George
have reason to believe otherwise. But this is not the only problem with the Costanza Maneuver. In addition to being unreliable, it is not a particularly feasible strategy. It is tough if not
impossible to approximate what the principle requires, much
less follow it to the letter. To show this, I want to start by explor-
ing the prospects for the Costanza Maneuver as a viable long-
term strategy.

In subsequent episodes, the Costanza Maneuver is all but for-
gotten. George wins initially, and although he keeps his job with
the Yankees awhile, he stops doing the opposite. The nature of
habit makes it clear why. Habits are patterns of learned

response to certain kinds of stimuli, patterns which become engrained over time. These patterns, like George's basic inclinations, can be hard to change. Long-standing habits especially can be reverted to far too easily, before and even after new habits are formed. Notice what happens later in the episode, when Elaine gets evicted:

GEORGE: Well, you could move in with my parents.

ELAINE: Was that the *opposite* of what you were going to say, or was that just instinct?

GEORGE: Instinct.

ELAINE: *Stick* with the opposite.

Still, habits can be changed, though when they are they tend to change other habits as well. The more one does the opposite, the more one becomes habituated to it, and the more one becomes habituated to it, the more "natural" the behavior becomes. But the more natural the behavior becomes, the more one is so inclined, and being inclined *that* way means *not* being inclined the way the Costanza Maneuver requires.

So either George lacks the right stuff to do the opposite over the long haul, or he has it, and the nature of habit would defeat him anyway. Over the long haul, the Costanza Maneuver would either upset the upset mind it relies on, or leave it altogether untouched. Either way, it fails to be a viable long-term strategy. But maybe doing the opposite would eventually lead to *recognizably* prudent impulses. Maybe George's commitment to the principle would gradually die out as the learning curve increased. Maybe the Costanza Maneuver would set aright inveterately wrong impulses. Maybe, but highly unlikely given how unreliable the strategy is in the first place.

Two things bear mention. One, even if the Costanza Maneuver is not a feasible strategy in the long run, that does not mean it is not feasible in the short run. Two, a rational strategy need not be long-term feasible. Take kamikaze pilots. It might be rational to fly one's plane into an enemy ship, especially if that is the best available means of attack. Suicide is hardly a viable long-term strategy, but it may still count as rational. Unfortunately for George, the rationality of the Costanza Maneuver is even less plausible than that of the kamikaze pilot.

Impulse Problems

One of the reasons the Costanza Maneuver is not a feasible strategy, even in the short-term, is that George has impulse problems. His behavior is often erratic, impulsive, random, ill-considered, if considered at all. True, in this episode he seems to have the wherewithal to oppose such impulses. Witness his unusual restraint as, in the following scene, he is driving Victoria to the movies:

> VICTORIA: Hey watch it! He just cut you off! Did you see that?

> GEORGE: Take it easy. Take it easy. It's not the end of the world.

Typically such restraint is impossible for George. It's just not in his character, and the Costanza Maneuver doesn't change that one bit. That he would be capable of such restraint, even in the short-term, is not something we have—or that he has—reason to expect.

Another problem is that George is prone to *akrasia,* or weakness of will. Not only does he often act on impulse before giving thought to the matter at hand, impulse often overpowers his better judgment. An amusing sort of fear and trembling is George's trademark, and it breeds weakness in the face of choices he knows to be prudent but never makes. This should be familiar enough to fans of the show, but look to the complement of *Seinfeld* episodes for all the evidence you need.

Not only does George know he has these problems, he should know that they would surely, if not for a great stroke of luck, confound his efforts to do the opposite. One problem I have not mentioned is that George is often paralyzed when confronted by the call to action, a problem of absent impulse. So really he has three confounding impulse problems. These are psychological, but deep as they are, they pale in comparison to what really makes the Costanza Maneuver unfeasible.

Indeterminacy of the Opposite

What really makes the Costanza Maneuver unfeasible is the indeterminacy of the opposite. To say something is indeterminate means that you cannot tell what it is. Many philosophers think the truth-value of the statement 'God exists' is indeterminate, because there seems no way we could determine whether the statement is true or false. Whether, as a matter of fact, it is true or false is (apparently) independent of whether we can discover this fact. When I say the opposite is indeterminate, I do not necessarily mean that actions lack opposites. Many do, but the point is: whether or not an action has an opposite, George cannot often, if ever, discover what it is.

An example will illustrate what I mean. Imagine George finds himself wanting to say something. What should he do? Should he say nothing? That would seem to be the opposite of saying something. Should he negate what he wants to say?—"These pretzels are *not* making me thirsty!" Should he say what he wants, but change the tone from sincere to sarcastic?—"That's a *great* parking-space, baby!" Should he, where possible, invert what he wants to say?—"I *love* the Drake." All of these are plausible candidates for the opposite. But which is the right one? If you think about it, for all, or at least most actions, there are many plausible candidates for what would constitute the opposite. None stands out as best, and this means trouble if you are after *the* opposite.

It is not just that the opposite is often if not always indeterminate. George *knows* this, as do Jerry and Elaine. If George had reason to think otherwise, he might be right to think the Costanza Maneuver feasible. For contrast, see how George recounts, with great excitement, his success with Victoria:

> GEORGE: I tell you this, something is happening in my life. I did this opposite thing last night. Up was down. Black was white. Good was—
>
> JERRY: —bad.
>
> GEORGE: Day was—
>
> ELAINE: —night.
>
> GEORGE: Yes!

But actions seldom fit into neat, determinate oppositions like up/down, black/white, good/bad, and night/day. (Historical note: ancient philosophers loved opposites. Hot/cold and wet/dry fascinated them no end.) What is the opposite of ordering tuna on toast, with coleslaw and coffee? Certainly not chicken on rye, with potato salad and tea. Notice what goes on in the following exchange:

> JERRY: You know, chicken salad is not the opposite of tuna. Salmon is the opposite of tuna, 'cause salmon swim against the current, and the tuna swim with it.
>
> GEORGE: Good for the tuna.

George quite obviously knows that his order is not a plausible candidate for the opposite. What's more, he doesn't care. Jerry ribs him, and he replies with sarcasm, well aware his order was a mere alternative. But would anything else be a better candidate?

Another problem is that for George to pull the maneuver at all he must know, before acting, what his inclinations are. If he does not, he cannot very well do the opposite. And George is often unaware of his inclinations until after he acts. Most of us have much milder forms of this tendency. Sometimes we want to do something, we know not what, and so we try out various possibilities. If the desire remains unsatisfied, we know we have guessed wrong. But if it becomes satisfied, we know we have guessed right. George has this in spades. In fact, it is often because he has no inclinations, or has them unawares, that George makes a neurotic mess of straightforward alternatives.

So the opposite is indeterminate not only because actions usually don't fit into nice, clean oppositions, but also because there is—frequently enough—the further indeterminacy of George not knowing what he wants to do. Aware of this, George is in no position to bet on the Costanza Maneuver being feasible, just as he is in no position to bet on its being reliable. It cannot be rational, then, for him to do the opposite, not only because the Costanza Maneuver is both unreliable and unfeasible, but because George knows this to be true.

[Cue Bass]

Looking at his success with Victoria, and in the job-interview, it might seem that the Costanza Maneuver at least counteracts

George's impulse to lie, making him a sort of virtue-mimic, which could after all be rational. But George does not tell Victoria the truth, he discloses it, and his confessional pride in the interview is pretty clearly hollow. Both involve truth-telling, fair enough, but the involvement is accidental. Notice how the tirade at Steinbrenner is patently a put-on, a *lie*, as are most of George's efforts. The Costanza Maneuver is not a reliable enough way to mimic virtue. The writers are rightly cynical in making it hard to pin George's success on any virtue, moral or rational, mimicked or real.

It still might seem pragmatically justified for George to *try* the opposite, for this may be less unreliable than his usual tactics. If you are going to bet, bet craps, because craps gives you the best odds. But the point is, you need not bet at all. Limited as he is, George can avail himself of countless strategies, many of them surely better than both the usual and the opposite. Besides which, is it at all plausible that being rude to Steinbrenner is a better job-getting tactic than obsequious politeness? Hardly. How about moderate deference, then? The opposite simply is not as good as George's usual, and both are significantly worse than other available strategies. That is where the humor lies—not as good, works better.

What would it take for the Costanza Maneuver to be a good strategy? Well, George would need something like a woe-tracking mechanism, something that always inclined him to what he should not do, where what he should not do has an obvious opposite. Setting aside the indeterminacy of opposites, there are two reasons why such a scenario could not work, even in the twilight zone of *Seinfeld*. First, much as we want to believe him, George's self-analysis is false. Many of his inclinations are fine: he eats (inclusively) when hungry, pays his diner bills, manages to keep friends in spite of himself, and so forth. Second, such a mechanism would have to come from neuroses so extreme that, if George tried to oppose them, they would doubtless outwit him, and feed him not the wrong inclinations to oppose, but the right ones.

George is a loser, and the Costanza Maneuver is merely a ploy to get away with avoiding significant questions about his own character—the shortcutter's shortcut, and we love him for it. He is lucky to gain some insight into his nature, however superficial, along with the means to counteract it, however spurious. More than that, he is lucky to be so pathetic that the Costanza Maneuver would occur to him at all, much less work. But the strategy is fraught with many difficulties, as we have seen, too many to make it viable. Is it rational to do the opposite? No, but even a blind squirrel can find a nut.[4]

---

[4] For helpful discussion, and for comments on earlier drafts, I thank Bob Bright, Larry Holt, Bill Irwin, Rhonda Martens, and Carl Matheson.

10
Peterman and the Ideological Mind: Paradoxes of Subjectivity[1]

NORAH MARTIN

> People want things that are hard to find. Things that have romance, but a factual romance, about them. . . . Clearly, people want things that make their lives the way they wish they were.
>
> —J. Peterman, *The J. Peterman Company Owner's Manual*

> [I]n contemporary societies, cynical distance, laughter, irony are, so to speak, part of the game. The ruling ideology is not meant to be taken seriously or literally.
>
> —Slavoj Zizek, *The Sublime Object of Ideology*

Those who watch the television comedy *Seinfeld* are aware that in the seventh season Elaine got a job writing copy for the catalogue clothing company, J. Peterman, a company better known for its narratives of clothing than for the clothing itself.[2] In this

---

[1] Thanks to Emily Zakin for numerous conversations about Lacan and for comments on an earlier draft of this paper. Thanks also to the many people with whom I have discussed *Seinfeld*, especially Jason Holm.
[2] For those who still don't know—J. Peterman is a real catalogue clothing company based in Lexington, Kentucky. Its catalogue, "The J. Peterman Owner's Manual," as on *Seinfeld*, contains narratives and line drawings.

essay I show the way in which J. Peterman's appearance on *Seinfeld* can be used to understand how ideology functions both through irony and through cynicism. Cynicism is, as will become clearer in the course of this essay, characterized by a naive belief in ultimate reality outside the illusions presented by ideology. Irony, on the other hand, involves the reduction of reality itself to a fiction. We will see this at two levels. On the first level we see why Peterman's appearance turns out to be good advertising, not in spite of, but rather *because* it makes us aware of the absurdity of the catalogue's premise, namely that people would prefer to read stories than see photographs of the clothing they are going to buy. If one were a cynic, one would sneer at the fanciful narratives (as indeed Elaine does), but if one is an ironist one laughs at the fact that one knows that the narratives in the catalogue are silly and yet one is still taken in by them. One still wants to be the person described in the narratives. One buys the clothing. The second level has to do with the Peterman character himself and the way in which he is like us. What Peterman ultimately reveals to us is that the Subject, the coherent and unified self, is constituted and maintained through ideology. In this revelation the ironic attitude extends beyond the world to oneself.

Ideology

Peterman's presence on *Seinfeld* could be seen to exemplify what Slavoj Zizek, a Marxist Lacanian,[3] calls "performative ideology." By "performative ideology" Zizek means a form of ideological consciousness in which we know that we are dealing with a fiction, but in which that fiction nonetheless regulates our actual real behavior. In other words, although we know that we are dealing with a fiction, we regulate reality as though the fiction were real. Ironically, in doing this we *make* the fiction real. Zizek uses the example of money. When people use it, they know that there is nothing magical about it. It is simply a means of exchange that gives the one who has it the right to certain

---

[3] Zizek is a philosopher who combines the social and political analysis of Karl Marx (1818–1883), particularly with regard to ideology, and the psychoanalytic theory of Jacques Lacan (1901–1981). This explosive combination allows him to use psychoanalysis to engage in a critique of culture and society.

things. On an everyday level, everyone knows that there are relations between people behind the relations between things. The problem is that people *act* as if money in itself is wealth. As Zizek says, "they are fetishists in practice, not in theory."[4] What they do not know or "misrecognize" is that in their activity they are guided by an illusion.

What is ideology? It is the system of ideas whereby we become conscious of ourselves, our lives, our world. In short, it is the system of ideas by which we become conscious of reality. Karl Marx draws a strict distinction between the actual conditions of life—the economic structure of society which is society's real foundation—and the "legal and political superstructure" or the "definite forms of social consciousness" by which we become aware of the foundation, albeit it in an inverted or disguised way. Marx sometimes refers to ideology as being like a *camera obscura*.[5] The mode of production of material life (capitalism, for example) conditions the social, political and intellectual life process—the *ideology*—of society. Marx says, "It is not the consciousness of men that determines their being, but, on the contrary, their social being that determines their consciousness."[6] We are conscious of ourselves, our lives, our world, through ideological forms.

For Marx, of course, there is an extra-ideological reality—the real material forces that govern our existence. For later theorists, this is, at best, not so clear. For psychoanalyst Jacques Lacan, we deal with the Symbolic Order (for example capitalism, liberal democracy, or patriarchy) in a fictional way. In other words, we believe that our world *makes sense*, is coherent, unified and consistent. However, this is a belief in an illusion. In believing in it we are averting our gaze from the gaps, the lack of consistency and coherence, and the raw power of the symbolic order. We

---

[4] Slavoj Zizek, *The Sublime Object of Ideology* (London: Verso, 1989), p. 31.

[5] A *camera obscura* is a concave mirror into which is reflected a scene from the outside through a series of mirrors, rather like a periscope. The effect is of seeing the outside from which one has just come, only everything is, as it were, "the same, yet different." Things are inverted, but it is hard to detect, and that is why it seems eerie. For further discussion of ideology, see Karl Marx, *The German Ideology* in David McLellan ed., *Karl Marx: Selected Writings* (Oxford: Oxford University Press, 1977), pp. 159–191.

[6] Karl Marx, "Preface to *A Critique of Political Economy*," in David McLellan ed., *Karl Marx: Selected Writings* (Oxford: Oxford University Press, 1977), p. 389.

are always dealing with a fiction because we always have, and need to have, an Imaginary relation to the Symbolic Order. In this sense, ideology *constitutes* our reality. Without it we can't have coherent, consistent experience. This is what Lacan means when he says that "reality is structured like a fiction."

I Laugh, Therefore I Buy

The way in which ideology functions may become more clear if we consider the distinction between cynicism and irony. We are all familiar with cynicism. Indeed, people often point to *Seinfeld* as a paradigm case of cynicism. *Seinfeld* is cynical in that its very premise is to point out the way in which we all participate in absurd social rituals, like bringing wine (not Pepsi or RingDings) when we are invited to someone's house for dinner, even if we don't drink wine. *Seinfeld* reveals what we already know: that we do it because of the power society seems to have over us, because of the rules that govern us, but of which we are not usually even fully conscious, not because of any real desire to do these things. We laugh as we see ourselves in the characters. We recognize the absurdity of these things that we do, and yet we all continue to do them. The stance of the cynic is to point out the inauthenticity of such behavior. The cynic believes that in doing that s/he is freed from the fetters of such social rules and rituals, freed from oppressive ideology.

When we look at the role of the J. Peterman Company, at Mr. Peterman himself and at Elaine's relation to them, however, we see something more than the cynicism we have come to expect. We cease to be cynics and begin to be ironists.

The cynic correctly believes that we deal with fictions, but s/he incorrectly concludes from this that the role of these fictions can be discounted. S/he believes that in recognizing the fiction s/he is free of it. But we can see that recognition of the fiction does not make us free. The fiction continues to regulate the behavior of the characters on *Seinfeld* as it does our own behavior. We laugh and we continue to behave as we always have. In fact we enjoy the behavior all the more for being able to laugh at it. We know it's not real, but we do it anyway. We can laugh at ourselves all we want, but we have not broken free. Indeed, it is in laughing at ourselves that we find ourselves doing it all the more, with that much more enjoyment. This is why Peterman's appearance on *Seinfeld* and our laughter at the absurdity of the premise of the catalogue is its best advertising. We enjoy the absurdity of buying clothes because of the "pointless drivel" which nonetheless has an effect on us.

Mr. Peterman, however, does not laugh at himself. Of all the characters on *Seinfeld*, none takes himself more seriously (in fact that's part of what is funny). Yet at the same time, he knows he's not *real*. He knows his whole life is the fiction in the catalogue. After all, he needs to buy Kramer's life stories because his life is only the one described in the catalogue, a life we know has been invented by people like Elaine. Mr. Peterman is completely a character. Every mundane experience he *does* have is narrated by him as though it was right out of his catalogue (as when he sees Sue Ellen Mishki disappear into an elevator wearing what was to become the "Gatsby Swingtop"). For him, every experience is a catalogue experience. Peterman knows none of it is real, yet he does not adopt a cynical distance, he is, ironically, committed to the fiction.

Elaine, however, does appear to have cynical distance. She refers to what she writes for the catalogue as "pointless drivel" (what the psycho from the mailroom might write couldn't be any worse than the pointless drivel they usually print, she says). We identify with Elaine. We know the descriptions in the catalogue are made up by people like her. We know (or at least strongly suspect) that the real Mr. Peterman (if there is one) isn't nearly as interesting as the one created in the catalogue. And we laugh. We laugh because none of that matters. We laugh and we look forward to getting the catalogue with the pointless drivel promising life "the way we wish it were."

Mr. Peterman, the Wicked Witch of the West, and Me

But why do we do this? To understand we must look more carefully at how Mr. Peterman is, strangely enough, the most realistic[7] character on *Seinfeld*. In him we can see the truth of subjectivity.

---

[7] I am frequently reminded of the line from Portland's Church of Elvis: "It's not real, it's *realistic*." Compare this to the challenge Malcolm McDowell finds in the new *Fantasy Island:* "We must be real, but not realistic" (*TV Guide*, October 10–16, 1998, p. 32).

Mr. Peterman is completely empty. He is nothing more than the narratives from his catalogue that make his life "the way he wishes it were." The catalogue is filled with vignettes from Mr. Peterman's fictional life. When he needs stories about his actual life, he has to buy someone else's, for he has none. Mr. Peterman's emptiness becomes sadly clear when we visit his apartment with Elaine and find nothing but a few pieces of plain furniture, blank walls and bare surfaces (what were we expecting to find?). In the case of Mr. Peterman (who, unlike Kramer, does not seem to have a first name[8]), when we, as it were, pull aside the curtain we don't find the pathetic humbug (which is what we find when we look at the real-life John Peterman who is a self-described failed businessman[9] with a way cool horseman's duster) but rather nothing at all. There is no Mr. Peterman beyond the catalogue narratives and the dashing exterior. He may accumulate things like JFK's golf clubs and a piece of the Duke and Duchess of Windsor's wedding cake (though presumably only for the catalogue, just as the real J. Peterman acquires things for the catalogue like the dress Rose was wearing when she met Jack on the Titanic), but that doesn't make him anything underneath.

In Lacanian/Zizekian terms, this makes him the subject *par excellence* and as such he reveals a fundamental truth, *the* fundamental truth, of us all. While we identify with the situations in which Jerry, Elaine, George, and Kramer find themselves, we also despise these characters (even while secretly loving them), but Mr. Peterman is us.

Whereas the typical Cartesian/Kantian subject, the self of the Modern Era, tends to be conceived of as being more like the Wizard of Oz—great and powerful on the outside, but really just the pathetic little man behind the curtain—Mr. Peterman is more like the Wicked Witch of the West—once the show or fiction is gone there is literally nothing left but clothing. In Mr. Peterman we see that the "inner self" or "real me" is nothing but an illusion, a primordial lie.[10] We need to believe in this illusion, but

---

[8] He is never referred to as anything but "Mr. Peterman" or "Peterman." (The J. of the real-life J. Peterman stands for John.)

[9] *The New York Times*, Business Section (16 December, 1997).

[10] In *The Indivisible Remainder* (London: Verso, 1996), Zizek says that the fundamental truth of Freud's teaching is that, "in the deepest kernel of our

it is just that. There is nothing at the center, as we can see if we look more carefully at the notion of subjectivity that emerges in the philosophical tradition that begins with Descartes.

The subject, the one who has experiences and thoughts, has been characterized by Lacan, Hegel, and Zizek as fundamentally a lack or "the self-identity of negativity." The subject is ultimately empty because it is the 'I' which stands behind all of our experiences, but is not and cannot itself be an object of experience as it is constituted by the predominant philosophical tradition stemming from Descartes and Kant. In this tradition, we find an empirical self that we experience, a 'me' with various characteristics, but the 'I' who is that 'me' has no experiencable qualities, no determinations. What is determinateless or indeterminate is nothing. The self that we know, then, the 'me', could be seen as a masquerade, a self 'put on'. Usually when we think of the self as a mask or masquerade we imagine that there is a *true* or *real* self behind the various masks, under the various costumes (even if, or perhaps especially if, it is only the pathetic little man behind the curtain). But this is an ideological illusion, an inversion if you will. Ultimately, there is nothing behind the mask or under the costume and so without them we are left with a pure void, just as the Wicked Witch of the West turned out to be nothing in herself—all that remained was a small pile of crumpled clothing and a hat. The 'real self', that is, a coherent, unified subject underneath the show, is a fiction. There is nothing but the show itself.

Jerry seems to see this fact only too well. In the same episode where Peterman buys Kramer's stories, "The Van Buren Boys," Jerry is dating a woman who *appears* to be perfect—attractive, funny, smart, and so forth—yet who is supposedly, in her essence, "a loser." Jerry is the only one who can't see this essence, the only one who operates solely on the level of appearance. When George asks, "Are you looking deep down at the person underneath?" Jerry responds, "No, I'm being as superficial as I possibly can." And of course that's all that Jerry can be. Unlike Peterman, Ellen, Jerry's girlfriend, has a "real self" beneath the surface to which Jerry, who can see only surfaces,

---

personality is a fundamental, constitutive, primordial lie, the *proton pseudos,* the phantasmic construction by means of which we endeavor to conceal the inconsistency of the symbolic order in which we dwell" (p. 1).

has no access. Kramer and George, however, can see her "loser" essence and conduct an intervention to get Jerry to see the truth. Jerry, confused, feels as if he is in a *Twilight Zone* episode. For him, the belief in this ideological illusion in which everyone else seems to be participating makes no sense. He lives in a world that is the same, yet different, from that of his friends, much like the experience of looking in a camera obscura. While George and Kramer believe in the myth of the coherent subject that underlies all experiences, Jerry seems to recognize that there is no such thing, or if there is, he can't see it. Peterman *demonstrates* that there is no such thing.

Mr. Peterman, like the Wicked Witch of the West, is nothing in himself. Without the narratives, the clothing and the "things that make life the way he wishes it were," there is no one. That's why he needs to *buy* his life story. His nothingness is all the more apparent if we consider the impossibility of his autobiography. An autobiography is the history of one's life written by oneself. Mr. Peterman's "autobiography" is made up of stories from Kramer's life written by Elaine. One might even see Mr. Peterman in this sense as being in the same position as a vampire trying to look at himself in the mirror.

Mr. Peterman thus represents us most completely. The 'I' is experienced by us as emptiness and as desire. In other words, as dissatisfaction. It is this constant dissatisfaction that creates what Marx identifies as "the proliferation of needs." Rather than recognizing that we lack, we constantly strive to "make our lives as we wish they were." The clothes in this case really do make the man (or woman). The narratives give us the sense of being the main character in a story far more interesting than the one we live. Now all I need to do to be that character is to buy the costume. I recognize the absurdity of it, but, ironically, I am still committed to the fiction. In fact, recognizing the absurdity only makes me more comfortable buying, as I at one and the same time recognize and refuse to recognize that there is nothing to me but the narratives. Kierkegaard, taking up a dictum attributed to the early Church Father Tertullian, said "I believe because it is absurd." Now we buy because it is absurd, but we have to if we are to maintain that fiction that gives us coherence, and we have to believe that it is absurd to avoid recognizing the lack of coherence, to avoid recognizing what Mr. Peterman shows us: that there is no unified subject beneath the appearance, that beneath the appearance there is no one at all, just as there is never anyone wearing the clothes in the line drawings in the catalogue.

The ironist recognizes this, but, necessarily, lives in the fiction. The ironist is in a much better position, however, than the cynic. Cynicism leaves one in an endless loop wondering why everyone doesn't understand the contradictions he sees. The ironist does understand this and also understands her own commitment to the fiction. The cynic is frustrated that it doesn't make sense that we participate in the fiction. The ironist simply smiles at it. She doesn't *experience* the lack of a coherent self and consistent world. If she did, she would be psychotic. Nonetheless, the ironist recognizes the necessity of the fiction and appreciates the absurdity.

11

The Secret of *Seinfeld's* Humor: The Significance of the Insignificant

JORGE J. E. GRACIA

One of the most paradoxical features of the *Seinfeld* phenomenon is the extraordinary popularity of the TV series, particularly with younger Americans, in the face of the insignificance of the topics around which the show revolves. How can a show that deals with what appear to be ordinary, everyday occurrences have such great appeal to a generation of Americans that seems to thrive on sex, violence, and catastrophe? The sex on *Seinfeld* is tame and the violence nonexistent. So, what is the secret of its success? The answer, of course, has to do with the nature of comedy and its opposite, tragedy.

Comedy, Tragedy, and *Seinfeld*

Why do we laugh, and why do we cry? Everybody knows that we laugh at what is funny and we cry at what is sad, but no one yet has come up with an acceptable theory of what is funny and what is sad. Every day we experience things that make us laugh and things that make us cry, and there are persons—actors, movie directors, authors—who seem to know how to cause both. The success of movies, TV shows, and fiction in general surely depends on whether they make us laugh or cry. What is it, though, that brings about these effects? It is very difficult to say. The problem is that, as St. Augustine observed about time, we seem to know what it is until we ask about it.

There is no scarcity of things that cause us to laugh and cry, and similarly, there is no scarcity of views and attempts to explain why we do so. This is not a case in which a lack of examples could contribute to the difficulty in explaining the facts. Of course, along with everyone else, I do not know *the* satisfactory answer, and frankly, at the moment I am not interested in it. Indeed, it would be quite boring to go through and examine the many theories that have been proposed to explain the funny and the sad. That is better dealt with in learned treatises and doctoral dissertations which collect dust in impressive libraries.

My task here is different. I am going to suggest one way of distinguishing the funny and the sad, without claiming that this is the only way to do so, that is, that it has perennial and universal validity. I leave such inflated claims for more sober treatments that seek scientific accuracy. After all, there is something incongruous about discussing the funny and the sad scientifically, for these are matters of emotion and feeling, of the heart if you will, rather than of science and the intellect.

The thesis I am going to illustrate, since I will not be mounting a defense properly speaking, is that we laugh at something because we see in it the significance of the insignificant, and that we cry at something else because through it we grasp the insignificance of the significant. Doesn't this formula sound impressive? It is meant to, although in fact I want to do more than to impress you. I want you to see something that I think I have grasped with some clarity. So, what do I mean by this pedantic formulation? Actually nothing pedantic. Or even very profound. Not even something new. It could not be very profound because if it were, it could not describe something with which we are so frequently and closely acquainted; it could not be new because something experienced so frequently could not have been overlooked in human history.

I mean to suggest that one of the reasons we laugh at a play, a show, or a book is that in it we see ourselves in a new light. All of a sudden we consider ourselves, our every day idiosyncrasies, manners, ways, and customs, the peculiarities that we generally do not notice but that permeate our existence, presented for what they are, regularities of daily living that pass us by as insignificant and yet have significance. A good comedy usually makes these come alive. Comedy is about what is ordinary, but it has to do not with accepting it as ordinary, but rather with seeing it as extraordinary. Here lies the key to success in comedy, and here lies the secret of humor in *Seinfeld.*

This series, like other successful comedies, attracts attention by capturing the significance of the insignificant. *Seinfeld* is not about important events in the lives of the protagonists; it is about what no one would consider important. In one of its most self-reflective moments, the show acknowledged this point: "It is about nothing," says the Executive of NBC who is considering producing it. Yet, the aim of the series is precisely to bring out these commonplaces. In doing so, it underscores that they are pertinent in ways that we never thought they were, and certainly in ways the characters themselves do not think they are. The portrayal of an event, or peculiarity, itself does not include the realization by the characters of what the audience realizes. The players continue to regard it as unimportant, but the audience, which sees itself through the characters immersed in the situation, realizes its relevance.

The case of the sad, what makes us cry, is just the opposite. A tragedy is not concerned with what is common and unimportant in our everyday lives, but rather the reverse. The subject matter of tragedy is momentous: love, death, betrayal, vice, virtue, pain, injustice, cruelty, revenge. Do I need to continue? The list is long, but anyone can easily distinguish these themes from those of comedy. No tragedy has ever been written about the sale of a van, mail delivery, or non-fat yogurt. And the same can be said about the characters of the play. In a piece intended to make you sad, the characters are, as the saying goes, "larger than life." In matters of sadness, we generally deal with heroes and villains, with victims and ogres.

The aim of a tragedy is not to underscore the significance of an event or character. This is assumed and evident. Too much literary criticism takes for granted that this is in fact what tragedies are aimed to do. No. The sad makes us see precisely that what we regard as significant and important is in some ways insignificant. Our will, our love, our cruelty, are, in the general scheme of things, unimportant. The gods have more momentous matters with which to concern themselves. In tragedy, then, as in comedy, our world is turned upside down. The order of our values and priorities is reversed. We learn that our beliefs do not hold, and a revision of them, a correction in our understanding of the way things are, must take place. But in tragedy, unlike in comedy, we do not laugh, because this realization involves the shattering of what we hold dear. Whereas comedy reveals to us the relevance of much in our lives to which we pay no attention, tragedy shows us that what we regard as important is not really so. The first teaches us a lesson without pain; the second makes us learn a shattering truth.

Comedy, unlike tragedy, focuses on what we ordinarily regard as insignificant because it is in this that the follies, absurdities, and idiosyncrasies of cultures are revealed. In death, suffering, catastrophes, great vices and virtues, crimes, and the like—which are the stuff out of which tragedy is made—the core of human nature is made evident. Human behavior at this level is the same or very similar, and cultural differences appear only as thin veneers that lack import. When it comes to comedy, on the contrary, it is the innocuous, everyday customs, attitudes, and events that take precedence, revealing as they do, the contradictions, paradoxes, and relativity of different cultures. This is one reason why comedy dates more easily than tragedy.

"The Outing": Queering *Seinfeld*?

In the episode known as "The Outing," we initially see George and his current romantic interest, Alice, sitting in George's car while he unsuccessfully tries to break up with her. Next, Elaine, George, and Jerry are sitting at a booth in the coffee shop. They are discussing George's failed attempts at breaking up with Alice. Jerry gets up and goes to the phone to talk with someone at New York University. He has an appointment with a reporter from the student newspaper who wishes to interview him about his comedy act. He does not know what the reporter looks like and has been waiting for some time, but he learns the reporter has already left for the interview. He comes back to his friends frustrated.

The usual give and take between them leads to a humorous discussion about who is the most unattractive world leader. The contest is between Brezhnev, De Gaulle, and Lyndon Johnson, but Golda Maier wins in Elaine's book. Two girls sitting behind Jerry and George are laughing at the conversation and Elaine notices. After informing Jerry and George *sotto voce,* she decides to play a trick on them. "Just because you two are homosexuals, so what?" And she goes on. "You should come out of the closet and be openly gay already." Jerry is appalled, but George plays along. He looks at Jerry: "So what do you say? You know you will always be the only man I'll ever love."

The girls in the next booth continue to laugh. But Jerry does not want to play. George urges him to join in, and Jerry responds by saying George would have fit right into the scene in Berlin in 1939, goosestepping by, "Come on, Jerry, come along." There is also another reason he does not want to go on with the farce. Many people think he is gay. Why? Because he is "thin, single, and neat." Elaine adds: "And you get along well with women." Which George says leaves him out. The latter part of the conversation, of course, has not been heard by the girls, one of whom is the reporter Jerry is supposed to meet. She has gone to the phone to see if she can speak with Jerry. Jerry and George go to the bathroom together and on the way pass the reporter, who gets a good look at them.

Two things stand out in the restaurant scene that are echoed in the rest of the episode. First, the insignificance of the situation. There is nothing weighty about it. Three friends are pretending to be something they are not in order to play a trick on some people who are eavesdropping on their conversation. The aim is to have a bit of fun. Second, they are working with the social stereotype of the male homosexual: thin, single, and well-liked by women. The first makes us feel comfortable—we are not dealing with anything that should be of real concern. Nothing important is happening; nothing serious is being discussed. The second makes explicit society's view of male homosexuals. We can laugh because we are confronted with something familiar, unproblematic, unimportant. And we do laugh because we are confronted with a stereotype we use, but of which we are not often conscious. We see the caricature we impose on male homosexuals in the light of a situation where nothing really bad can happen. We can safely look at our peccadilloes as mere peccadilloes.

Next we find George and Jerry in Jerry's apartment; Jerry is waiting for the reporter, who has finally connected with him. When Jerry opens the door, the reporter realizes that he is one of the guys at the restaurant, and although Jerry thinks he has seen her before, he is not sure where. She is embarrassed. George is introduced and we are led to believe that she sees here an opportunity of interviewing two gays, something more socially interesting than just the standard interview with a comedian. She wants to talk to George too, of course. But in their ignorant bliss, Jerry and George are puzzled at this. Why should she want to talk to George?

They sit down to do the interview, which the reporter wants to tape. George does not like this idea, because his voice always "sounds so high and whiney" on tape. He waves his arms while he says it. All of this confirms the reporter's belief that Jerry and George are gay. The confusion goes deeper. What do you do besides comedy? Jerry says he is working with George on a pilot for NBC. "So you also work together?" The "also" makes clear that she takes for granted a relationship between the two, but Jerry and George can't understand. What does she mean?

Further developments confirm the reporter's belief. George is worried about a pear he is going to eat. Has Jerry washed it? Yes, he says. But George doubts it. Exasperated, Jerry answers, "So wash it!" To which George answers by addressing the reporter: "You hear how he talks to me?" What could be more natural between two lovers? The reporter: "You should hear the way my boyfriend talks to me!" Now Jerry is really puzzled: "What?" But the moment passes and George is on a roll. He asks the reporter what she thinks about the shirt he is wearing, because Jerry does not like it. The audience knows what the reporter is thinking but also that the shirt was a gift from Alice.

Several things are going on here that make us laugh. For one, we are replaying and expanding on the stereotype: The pear incident has to do with neatness; the shirt incident with an unusual preoccupation with clothes; the comment about the high-pitched and whiney voice, together with exaggerated gestures, point to social markers for male homosexuals; and the complaining is supposed to reveal a standing, long-term relationship. Contributing to the fun, of course, is that we know the assumptions under which each party is operating. And we also project ourselves into the situation.

The action continues. The reporter asks Jerry and George how they met, and Jerry tells her in the locker room of a gym. George corrects him: Actually it was a class. George was climbing a rope, burning his thighs because he kept slipping, and eventually fell on Jerry's head. At this point George grabs Jerry's ankle in a friendly gesture, which the reporter interprets as more than that. She is taking notes. She has a story. "Do you guys live together?" No. George has his own place. "Do your parents know?" Jerry is beginning to suspect that something is wrong, but George is oblivious. "My parents?" he responds, "They don't know what's going on!"

Suddenly, Jerry realizes the reporter is the girl in the restaurant. Wow! Now her questions fit. George and Jerry go into a panic. "Oh no! No!" And Jerry tries to explain: "We're not gay. *Not that there's anything wrong with that!*" And George, "No, of course not!" Jerry: "I mean it's fine if that is who you are." George: "Absolutely!" Jerry: "I have many gay friends." George: "My father is gay." We laugh, and the reporter is not convinced. "I know what I've heard." George is desperate: "Do you want to have sex right now?" Do you want to have sex with me right now? Come on, let's go!" (George, proud of his overflowing heterosexuality, had earlier declared to Jerry that if he were a porno star his name would be "Buck Naked.") Then Kramer comes in and seals their fate: "I thought we were going to take a steam!" "No, no steam!" is the response of the trapped duo. And Kramer: "I don't want to sit there naked all by myself!"

By this time we are rolling with laughter. The gay stereotype is confirmed and developed by almost everything that happens in this scene. The places where gays meet: gyms. The places they frequent: steam baths. The need to keep knowledge of their sexual orientation from family. The familiarity of touching between males. All these are things society expects of gays. But now we also get a picture of the hypocritical attitude of society toward them. Jerry and George are in a panic about being thought to be gay, and try to do all they can to deny they are while at the same time insisting, incongruously, that there is nothing wrong with being gay. "I have many gay friends." Which reminds everyone of the other line: "Some of my best friends are black."[1] "It's fine if that's what you are." But then why the desperation? Why the panic? Why the extraordinary efforts to deny it? If there is nothing wrong with being gay, why are Jerry and George so worried about being taken for gays? We

---

[1] See "The Diplomat," for George's desperate search to establish that he has black friends.

are not worried about being taken for stockbrokers when in fact we are lawyers, or about being thought French, when we are in fact Italian.

The well-known, bigoted, formulas keep pouring out. The contrast between what Jerry and George say, and their extraordinary attempts to rectify a situation they consider appalling, is incongruous and makes us laugh because we recognize ourselves in it. The ways we act and our beliefs are often at odds, and we are generally unaware of this fact. Those who are not gay identify with Jerry and George; those who are gay and in the closet see their own panic at being discovered; and those who are gay and out of the closet realize the paradoxes of their social situation. Everybody laughs because we all get a picture of our well-intentioned bigotry.

The rest of the show works out the implications of the confusion about the sexual orientation of Jerry and George. First comes the fear that the reporter will publish something about it in the paper. Other attempts are made to disabuse her of the misconception under which she is laboring. In the first attempt Jerry talks to her, but he is using a two-line phone he gets as a birthday gift from Kramer. (Elaine had originally gotten him the same thing, but upon learning that Kramer gave him the phone she buys Jerry *The Collected Works of Bette Midler*.) While he is on the phone with her, George calls, and Jerry tells him that she has just told him she is not going to play the homosexual angle in the article. What a relief! So he adds: "I guess we fooled her." But the phone is not working properly and the reporter hears what he says to George. George informs Jerry he could hear what Jerry was saying, so they realize the reporter heard Jerry and that is why she has hung up. Obviously, they are back where they started, only worse, because now the reporter thinks they have been trying to deceive her. Their initial relief turns into terror. George: "Now she thinks we're gay! *Not that there's anything wrong with it.*" To which Jerry, even in a state of complete desperation, adds that people's personal sexual preferences are their own business.

George and Jerry enlist Elaine's help, and she goes to see the reporter to try to change her mind. But the meeting backfires because of Elaine's stubborn resistance to taking off her coat. Jerry expresses his worries to Elaine and George at the coffee shop: "Now everyone at NYU thinks I'm gay. *Not that there's anything wrong with that!* And all because Elaine did not take off her coat. The article is out but they have not seen it. At this point two guys at the counter call Jerry's attention to an article in the New York Post about him. Shock! The story from the NYU paper has been picked up by other papers. "I've been outed and I wasn't even in!" George: "Now everyone's going to think we are gay." He is almost crying. And Jerry: *"Not that there's anything wrong with that!"*

Back at the apartment they read the article, where the stereotype is played out again. From this moment on the episode is about Jerry and George trying to contain "the damage" on their friends and family. Kramer: "I thought we were friends!" Jerry: "It's not true!" But Kramer does not believe him. Stop the masquerade. "You're thin, late thirties, single." Jerry retorts; "So are you!" To which Kramer shrinks in horror at the implication that he might also be gay—he does not consider the possibility that his description does not imply gayness—and leaves in a hurry.

George answers the phone: "Mrs. Seinfeld?" She is strangely stunned at the sound of George's voice answering the phone at her son's apartment. This makes George remember his mother and he runs out in a rush. Jerry takes the phone and denies the story. In the meantime, we see his father blaming Jerry's mother. "It was those damned culottes you made him wear when he was five!" The mother is, of course, understanding: *"Not that there's anything wrong with that, Jerry."*

George's turn with his mother is at the hospital, where she was unhappily delivered, having fallen off the toilet when she read the story. She complains that she doesn't know her son any longer. Jerry, she can see: "He is so neat and thin. *Not that there's anything wrong with it."* Again we see the same social duplicity that was evident in the attitude of Jerry and George present in Kramer and Jerry's parents. They repeat that there is nothing wrong with being gay, but they are appalled at appearing to be one (Kramer) or having children who are so (Jerry's parents, George's mother). And they all share the same social stereotype.

While George is talking to his mother, another dimension of the issue is explored. A tall, handsome, male nurse comes into the room to give a sponge bath to the male patient in the next bed. We see George's expressions as he looks at the shadows of the nurse and the patient while they talk. Patient: "I fell asleep." Nurse: "Let me help you off with that. I'll slip it over your head."

Patient: "Yeahhh . . . that feels really good!" There is worry, and even terror, in George's eyes at the thought that maybe there could be something to the story. George's homophobia is clearly fueled by the possibility of a latent homosexual attachment to Jerry. Incidentally, this angle is also explored in "The Cartoon," in which George is dating a woman everyone says looks like Jerry. This creates a crisis for George, who thinks that perhaps he is secretly, unconsciously, in love with Jerry. Oh, no![2]

Back at the coffee shop a soldier comes to tell Jerry that he was inspired by his action and is coming out of the closet even if he has to leave the service. This is odd, even surreal. Jerry is becoming more and more self-conscious; he is appalled by and won't accept George's invitation to *Guys and Dolls,* a gift for Jerry's birthday. George gets mad. "Everything is tainted now." "Would you keep your voice down?" says Jerry. But George begins to shout. The waiter reacts by telling them: "If you boys cannot control yourselves, then I'm afraid I'm going to have to ask you to leave." Another addition to the stereotype: Gays appear immature and do not exercise the same self-restraint heterosexual males do.

But there is a silver lining to every cloud. George suddenly realizes that when Alice reads the article, she will want to break up with him, something we know he has wanted from the beginning of the episode. Matters do not work out that easily, however. First, because when Alice reads the article, she doesn't get the point. So George has to tell her. "I'm gay. I'm a gay

---

[2] A very early episode, #18, "The Note," also deals with George's preoccupations with possible latent homosexuality. In this episode, George is concerned because "it moved" during a massage given to him by a man. Even earlier in "Male Unbonding," the question of how to end a male heterosexual relationship, has homosexual undertones. Other *Seinfeld* episodes dealing with homosexuality include, but are not limited to, "The Jacket" in which Elaine's father thinks George is gay and has his suspicions about Jerry, "The Beard" in which Elaine tries to get a gay man to "switch teams," "The Stall," in which George likes Elaine's "cool guy" boyfriend a little too much, "The Cheever Letters," in which a homosexual life at the cabin is revealed, "The Soup Nazi" and "The Puerto Rican Day," in which stereotypes are exploded with effeminate street toughs, "The Wig Master," in which Jerry is insulted when one gay man tries to pick up another gay man with whom he is sitting, and "The Smelly Car" in which Susan (who has become a lesbian since the break-up with George) temporarily loses her girlfriend to Kramer.

man. I'm very very gay, extraordinarily gay, steeped in gayness."
Second, because even then Alice does not believe him. "Ask
Jerry." "I will." George sees he is in trouble, because, of course,
Jerry is not going to confirm the story.

Next we see Jerry and the reporter (who reminds him of Lois
Lane) making out in Jerry's apartment. George barges in with
Alice and, in order to convince her that he is Jerry's lover, acts
offended, as if Jerry had betrayed him—and with a woman!
Confusion ensues, and the reporter leaves. Jerry goes after her:
"It's not true; it's not true. *Not that there's anything wrong* with
that." So Alice wants to know, and George finally concedes.
Then Kramer comes in with a handsome man and everybody
looks at him suspiciously. He realizes what is going on and
returns shortly after he leaves: "He's the phone man! *Not that
there's anything wrong with that."*

What's so Funny about That?

Now let us go back to my thesis: *Seinfeld* is funny because it
shows us the significance of the insignificant. The episode we
examined is about the attitude toward male homosexuals in
contemporary American society. This attitude has two sides to it.
First, the stereotype of the male homosexual. This involves age,
looks, habits, gathering places, behavior, relations with women,
and so on. Second, duplicity. Whereas no one who is educated
and middle class wants to be thought, or be, prejudiced against
gays, everyone is terrified at being thought, or being, gay.

We do not regard this attitude as anything momentous,
important, or significant. We "know" it is not going to end up in
the persecution of gays, precisely because we do not want to
see, or appear to see, anything wrong with being gay—as long
as it does not touch us, of course. Jerry and George are not
going to beat up gays outside gay bars, and they are going to
support social measures which protect gays. Society does not
regard their duplicity as something significant as it does with
death, disasters, betrayal, pain, virtue, injustice, and love. Yet,
the episode shows us precisely how significant it is by uncovering the paradox present in our social attitude toward gays and
making us realize the importance of what we normally do not
acknowledge. Is it true that, as the saying goes, "you are either
part of the problem or part of the solution"? Perhaps not;

perhaps this is a false dichotomy; but perhaps it is worth considering whether Jerry, George, and indeed each of us are part of the problem or part of the solution in assuring equal treatment for homosexuals. But that is not a subject I can even begin to address here. Rather, my purpose has been to explore the issue of *Seinfeld's* comic appeal. And this I have done.

Highlighting the significance of the insignificant is the secret of *Seinfeld's* humor. And, indeed, there is nothing wrong with it.

Act IV

Is There Anything Wrong with That?

12
Seinfeld and the Moral Life

ROBERT A. EPPERSON

Why must a person bring gifts when invited to a party? When dating, how long must one person wait after having sex before it is acceptable to break up with the other person? If an animal annoys you sufficiently, may you kill or kidnap it? Is it wrong to ask for a person's name after you've already kissed romantically? Are you responsible for a person's death by poisoning if you bought cheap wedding invitations with toxic glue? Are you responsible for finding a person a new job if you were instrumental in getting the person fired from the previous one? What are the obligations of friendship? What do adult offspring owe their parents? What are the limits of truth telling? What kind of loyalty does an employee owe her employer? What sorts of obligations, if any, exist between fellow citizens?

It should be obvious even to the most casual viewer of *Seinfeld* that one of the program's primary themes is proper conduct. In this respect it resembles much of what falls under the heading of "situation comedy" on television. Much of what is comic in such programs is the characters' attempts to act rightly in situations of limited information—both factual information and moral information, such as which moral principles are true, what moral terms mean, and so forth. This is what comedy shares with drama, and with narratives more generally.

What is unique about *Seinfeld*, and strikingly so, is the degree to which the principle characters are concerned with acting "rightly," as is shown by the regular consultation with each other as to what constitutes the right course of conduct in the many and various circumstances each faces.[1] Indeed, I take Seinfeld to be about right conduct, living the moral life in contemporary American society. In this essay I will discuss the notion of the moral life and its relation to happiness and a good life, and show how central this concern is to *Seinfeld*. As a result, I will in part be defending the program from the common charge that it merely depicts, albeit comically, the aimless lives of self-absorbed, superficial, immature, upper west side New Yorkers.

The Moral Life

Let me first articulate what I mean by the moral life, and then I will go on to point out why I think living such a life is of primary concern to the *Seinfeld* characters.

With very few exceptions, we each want to live well and be happy, and it is generally acknowledged, usually implicitly, that acting rightly is a necessary component of this life. Of course, there is some occasional difficulty in determining which of our available actions is the right one, but this takes place against a background of easy choices, cases in which there is no difficulty at all and in which we know all we need to know in order to do the right thing. For example, we seldom consider whether harming the innocent is morally permissible, whether acting against another's will through deception or force is OK, or whether we ought to help others when we easily can. It is against this clear picture that the problem cases stand out.

What makes a moral circumstance problematic is a lack of some relevant knowledge on the part of the agent or agents involved. In some cases what is not known is factual, empirical information such as whether capital punishment really is an effective deterrent to further crimes or whether pursuing this

---

[1] It is for this reason perhaps that the show's final episode struck a false note with many viewers, including myself. The principle characters regularly involve themselves in others' lives—Jerry with Babu the Pakistani restaurateur, Kramer aiding the homeless and walking for AIDS, George helping the busboy whom he caused to be fired—thus the charge that their sin is indifference is false on its face.

course of action really will maximize the benefit for those affected. In other cases the agent or agents are in a condition of uncertainty about moral information. Examples include: what makes a living thing worthy of full moral consideration, and whether a fetus is one of those kinds of things, and what features of a thing or what relations it has to others endow it with moral rights. The most difficult areas of moral knowledge are those about morality itself, such as which moral theory is correct and what moral terms like 'right' and 'wrong' mean.

A person aspiring to live a moral life, aside from having the standing desire or interest to act rightly, acknowledges this condition of uncertainty about his or her knowledge, especially about his or her moral knowledge. As I mentioned above, in most cases, knowledge of the most general moral information is unnecessary—I don't need to know the correct moral theory in order to know that, in the situation that confronts me, harming the innocent would be wrong, or that helping the needy would be morally praiseworthy, in the same way that I don't need to know the applicable physical law of motion to catch a ball. However, living the moral life requires recognizing that some moral cases are difficult and that one's lack of moral knowledge in such cases is precisely what makes them difficult. Difficult moral cases should be treated with modesty on the part of the moral agent. Thus the moral life includes the recognition that one's own current beliefs, generally, but more specifically, those about which action is right and which moral theory is correct, might, after all, be mistaken.

Contrast this with a conception which is often confused with the moral life, what I will call "the life of integrity." It is important to contrast integrity with the moral life, since much is often made of integrity in the public realm (in the form of "standing up for what one believes"), and one might argue that the *Seinfeld* characters are morally blameworthy largely because they have little or no moral integrity. Thus I want clearly to distinguish the two and show why, especially for morally flawed characters like those we are considering here, acting with integrity may not be an admirable trait. A person can be said to act with integrity when acting in a way consistent with his or her deeply held moral judgments, judgments about which actions are right or wrong and which objects are good or bad. We often say that a person has integrity when, in difficult moral circumstances, such a person acts according to his or her own standards even in the face of strong, and perhaps quite reasonable, criticism. The life of integrity can be said to consist of the life lived with a standing desire to act in accordance with one's own deeply held moral judgments.[2] It is for this reason that integrity is not an unconditional virtue, since one should recognize that one's own judgments may be mistaken. Where they are mistaken, acting on them "come what may" frustrates that wish to act rightly and, thus, makes the notion of living well, which includes acting rightly, impossible.

We can see more clearly the dangers of acting with integrity by considering the most common kinds of people who would most strongly value it. Foremost, of course, would be the dogmatist, acting on his or her accepted moral judgments despite what should be recognized as strong evidence that those judgments are mistaken. We can see this most prominently in a certain sort of religious or political zealotry where the deep conviction may be used in defending what would otherwise seem morally repugnant actions. Another advocate of integrity would be the moral relativist, acting with the conviction that moral error is impossible because morality is simply determined by an individual's judgment, in which case there is no room for error. The third kind of person who would sanctify integrity would be the moral nihilist, acting on his or her own judgments of conduct, convinced that there are no true moral principles or theories to be mistaken about. (Even the most casual viewer of *Seinfeld* recognizes that Jerry, George, Elaine, and Kramer are not dogmatists, nor relativists, nor nihilists about morally right conduct.)

By contrast to the types discussed above, a person aspiring to live the moral life wants to act in accordance with *the correct* moral theory, even if it differs from her current, deeply held, moral judgments. In some cases, we must recognize that the course of action that morality requires can be unsettlingly contrary to our own deeply held moral beliefs.[3] Living the moral

---

[2] I acknowledge Kramer's advice to George to "listen to your little man" in making a difficult moral decision. This sounds like advice to act with integrity. Tellingly, George responds that his "little man" doesn't know what to do.

[3] One need only follow the torturous route of the Just War Theory, proposed and defended so that Christians could, in some cases rightly, kill others,

life, then, requires acting with a type of modesty about one's moral judgments. Indeed, acting while acknowledging one's own moral fallibility seems a necessary condition for developing a good moral character.

The Pursuit of the Moral Life in *Seinfeld*

In what way then is this conception of the moral life of central concern to *Seinfeld*, and in what way is it the primary occupation of the program's principal characters? This may seem, on first consideration, a difficult case to make, given the widespread contention that the characters are generally conceited and superficial and that *Seinfeld* is a show governed by the policy, "no learning, no hugging." Making the case requires first that I say some things about what form the pursuit of the moral life must take.

Since the moral life is the life concerned with acting rightly, the pursuit of that life will be conducted in the sphere of action, in contrast with that of contemplation, devotion, or some other area of activity in which social interaction is restricted or otherwise limited. The moral life is not best pursued in isolation from society.

Aside from its social component, pursuing the moral life is a continuous activity, comprised largely of the otherwise mundane events of one's everyday waking existence. For most people, that life contains very little of what might be called "adventurous morality," those exotic events often used as examples in courses on moral philosophy involving saving fifty native inhabitants by killing one, or stealing bread to save one's ailing mother, *yada yada yada*. While some lives include many of these events, and most every life includes some of them, the great majority of lives simply involve common moral predicaments. These typically include such things as workplace conflicts, small family decisions, and complications involving friends, lovers, or animals. In other words, the very circumstances covered in a typical episode of *Seinfeld*.

---

though it directly conflicted with both Old and New Testament doctrines. St. Augustine goes so far as to argue that one can kill one's enemies without violating Jesus' command to love your neighbor, provided one kills with a loving spirit.

Thus, since the moral life is best pursued in circumstances of frequent social interaction involving predominantly common events and situations, the structural aspects of *Seinfeld* lend themselves neatly to a focus on right and wrong action. In fact, *Seinfeld* lends itself to moral consideration much more so than many other "challenging" dramas depicting the activities of law enforcement or institutional medical treatment, which are often praised as programs where difficult moral situations are presented. Actually, it is the very difficulty of many of the moral situations presented which makes such programs unhelpful as arenas for inquiry into morality and the moral life, more broadly.

Let's consider the claim that the characters in *Seinfeld* really are concerned with acting rightly and, through this concern, living a better life. It is uncontroversial, I think, to insist that leading a good life and being happy are pervasive concerns of the program's main characters. Often the sentiment is expressed that a character's current life is not meeting his or her conception of the good life, and this is mentioned with some regret, implying a desire that things be otherwise. It is just this circumstance which prompts George Costanza to adopt the odd, but not unwarranted, strategy of "doing the opposite" of what he would be inclined to do, since his life to that point is thought to be such a failure. Even the generally contented Jerry sometimes expresses the desire that his life be better and happier. Recall in one episode George and Jerry resolve to find spouses so as to "become men" and thus improve their lives. The characters recognize that the actions one chooses to perform are instrumental in bringing about the happiness or unhappiness of one's life. Thus, it is clear that the characters recognize the relation between action and the general condition of his or her life. Indeed, this is a continual source of reflection and anxiety for both George and Elaine, the two characters whose lives reflect the most discontinuity precisely because neither knows what to do.

Now let's get to the heart of the matter. Do the characters truly care to act rightly? As I have suggested, I think the answer is clearly and categorically that they do. What, perhaps, makes this difficult to see is that they do not make their moral decisions from a script, as it were. They do not consult the Bible or the Torah for moral guidance, they do not consider maximizing overall utility nor do they try to act on such universalizable moral principles, as divine command, utilitarian, or Kantian moral theories would recommend. Nor do they merely follow cultural conventions in making their moral judgments. Rather, they frequently insist that one do, or refrain from doing, a particular action because of its independent moral character, regardless of whether it is consistent with cultural norms. Kramer is especially noteworthy for this. Let's consider some examples. Kramer bluntly encourages a woman to get cosmetic surgery because (rightly) "somebody needed to tell her," and he imitates a detective to recover a stolen cheap statue from an intimidated thief rather than shrug it off and avoid the conflict. Jerry tries to track down a hit-and-run driver (who turns out to be beautiful, so he is unable to turn her in), and he agrees to visit a sick boy in a bubble rather than disappoint the boy's insistent father. In each of these cases the more conventional behavior would be to not get involved, or, in Kramer's case, to be more tactful, but the characters instead are motivated to do the actions because they judge the actions to be required by morality.

In addition to the apparent lack of any guiding theoretical outlook, the imperfection of the New York Four's moral characters may misleadingly suggest that they are not especially concerned with acting rightly. George Costanza is frequently petty, Cosmo Kramer is often insensitive, Jerry has moments of selfishness, and Elaine Benes is occasionally abrasive. (Perhaps surprisingly, it's just the characters' imperfections which make them especially endearing.) It is that their imperfections are so obvious that has suggested to many critics that the characters really are unconcerned with morality.

But it is the presence of imperfection of character that makes a concern for morality possible. That the characters have moral flaws and must act in the face of these flaws is what provides the possibility for interesting and problematic moral decision-making (as well as the comic foundation for many of the situations). As Aristotle famously insists, for the person of fully virtuous character acting rightly is easy and pleasurable, but for those who are not yet fully virtuous, acting rightly takes time and practice.[4] The practice of acting rightly often includes mis-

---

[4] In *Nichomachean Ethics,* book 2.

taken judgments. It is exceedingly obvious that the *Seinfeld* characters are not morally perfect, but this imperfection is what drives the concern with acting properly.

Some Considerations

The view I am proposing, that *Seinfeld* is largely about the main characters' attempts to live the moral life, might be the target of objections from several directions. I want to consider some of these.

First, the point has been made by some popular commentators that the program is primarily about manners, not about morals. Manners (or etiquette) are the set of principles for action in social situations providing guidance for "proper conduct," in the sense of socially acceptable conduct. Such principles are wholly conventional and may vary fundamentally from culture to culture or from subculture to subculture. Commentators observe that *Seinfeld* offers us a comic look at the etiquette of neurotic, single, white, New Yorkers in their mid-thirties. Manners are not morals, and thus there is no basis for the claim that Jerry, Elaine, and the others, are concerned with anything more than "fitting in" and acting properly in a relatively superficial sense.

While it is true that many of the circumstances that arise in *Seinfeld* are matters of etiquette, for example whether it is rude not to make cake available to guests after dinner, or whether one should tell the parents of a newborn that the baby is ugly, many of the circumstances are certainly matters of morality. Jerry's, as well as Elaine's, frequent sexual predicaments clearly fall under the scope of sexual morality (for instance, what are the right motives for having sexual intercourse?). George Costanza's adventures in the workplace provide textbook cases for business ethics concerns such as corporate loyalty, whistle-blowing, and sexual harassment. More general moral concerns are pervasive throughout the series, considerations about causing harm to others, honoring agreements and obligations, and a deep and abiding devotion to justice (both distributive and retributive) run through nearly every episode. (George often goes to great lengths to see that personal injustices are rectified.) The objection that the show focuses exclusively on manners is quite obviously false on its face.

Still, *Seinfeld* leads us to question the relation between manners and morality. Are they neatly separable? Though a full consideration of this is beyond the scope of this paper, I think it is clear that the two share some conceptual space. Consider that one general principle of etiquette is to minimize causing offense to others. This sounds very much like a consequentialist moral principle. The conventional aspect of such a principle would be in its application, given what various cultures find offensive. Another general principle of etiquette might be expressed as "treat others as they should be treated," which is very much a principle of justice. Thus, insisting that *Seinfeld* is at best a program about modern manners is not inconsistent with its being about morality as well.

The more serious objection to my claim that the characters are pursuing the good life through morally right action is that the characters really are morally degenerate, concerned primarily with their own welfare, often at others' expense, and thus are generally morally blameworthy and show no signs of regret or remorse. This charge against the program is actually the theme of its final episode. The characters are found guilty of not caring sufficiently about others, and are thereby sentenced to a year in jail, a punishment deserved, it is suggested, by their moral indifference (notice that it is not merely by their being rude or inconsiderate).

The best response to this objection is to be found in the details of *Seinfeld* episodes. It would be tedious to go through them, so I will speak to the general themes of each principal character's life in fashioning a reply.

Let's consider briefly each of the four—Jerry Seinfeld, George Costanza, Elaine Benes, and Cosmo Kramer—in ascending order of importance. Kramer is the least morally conflicted of the group. In many ways he is the type of person Plato depicts as being of right opinion about ethical matters, but without knowledge. His acts are often the right ones, though pretty clearly any account he may offer of what makes them right would be terribly unreliable.[5] The only recognizable moral advice he offers is "listen to your little man"—a kind of homunculus theory of

---

[5] Of course, Kramer's judgment is not infallible. The most obvious example of this is when he encourages George to park his car in a space reserved for the handicapped. The car is subsequently destroyed by a righteously angry mob.

moral decision making—and this is just the sort of advice a person who tends to choose well would give. Because of his generally reliable judgment, Kramer stands out as, and is routinely recognized as, the best moral agent of the four, and for this he has a kind of peace of mind the others lack.

Elaine Benes, on the other hand, is terminally disappointed with her life, and this is the result of her poor choices in work, romance, and living arrangements. Of all the characters, Elaine's life most clearly illustrates the widely held conviction that right action is necessary for living well and being happy. She struggles against her own indecisiveness, which typically results in frustration, thus her tendency towards irascibility and peevishness. It is this that is her major obstacle to acting rightly. However, it is also quite clear that this condition is one she wants to change.

The most morally conflicted character is certainly George Constanza. Because of his deeply flawed character, he is also often the most desperate to do what is right. His fundamental shortcoming is his pathological small-mindedness (indeed, aside from his girth, shortness and smallness describe his mode of existence, physically, psychologically, and morally). If any character is a candidate for the charge of lacking any concern for morality, it would be George. Yet, repeatedly, we see George trying to avoid harming others, occasionally even attempting to help others, trying to be truthful, trying to be just, albeit, because of his deep flaws, he often fails. But it is clear, I think, that he does care about acting in accordance with correct moral principles. Unfortunately, unlike Kramer, he is typically the man of wrong opinion about morality.

The lead character, Jerry Seinfeld, is the moral axis around which the other characters revolve. This is not to say that he is fully virtuous, but rather that he is the most fully realized moral agent of the four. By this I mean that he is neither fortunate in his judgment, like Kramer, nor is he deeply unfortunate in his judgement, like George, nor is he confused in his judgment, like Eliane. As such, he is the character with whom we feel the most moral identification—as his mother frequently asks, "How could anyone not like you?" This is shown clearly by the fact that Newman is Jerry's nemesis; Newman is the opposite of Jerry in nearly every respect: overweight, slovenly, conniving, tormented, malicious, and so forth. Jerry's main constitutional shortcoming is vanity, though in some respects this is under-standable. He is "thin, single, and neat," has amusing friends and frequent dates with attractive women; he is financially success-ful as a comedian—and confesses that he has never had another job. As Jerry himself points out, things always seem to work out for him—Kramer once calls him "Even Steven." Yet, with all this, he often recognizes that morality makes demands on him that he must meet, even when, as is often the case, those demands are contrary to his desires. Even so, Jerry, like each of the other characters, is not a person inclined to melancholic contempla-tion of the requirements of the moral law (a tough trait to work into a comedy, Woody Allen aside). But that he is not is no evi-dence that he, or the other characters, is unconcerned with act-ing rightly.

Conclusion

I have argued that *Seinfeld* is largely about characters attempt-ing to live a moral life. The moral life, I claimed, is the life lived with a standing desire to act in accordance with true moral prin-ciples, as opposed to the life of integrity which is often confused with the moral life. By way of establishing this view I have said a bit about how we might expect the moral life to be pursued best, through frequent social interactions of a rather everyday sort, as opposed to through acting in the face of great calamities or in especially traumatic circumstances. Thus, the setting for *Seinfeld*—the social lives of thirty-something singles living in Manhattan—is fitting for its characters to pursue the moral life actively through right action. The main characters really do dis-play a concern with acting properly. Making the case is difficult given the widespread belief that the characters are at best unsympathetic to moral considerations, and at worst indifferent to them. Rather than go through a tedious list of the details of the program (those are best captured through viewing), I have sketched the respective moral predicaments of each character and argued that it was just their moral imperfections which gen-erates their concerns for acting rightly and being happy.

Seinfeld is a television comedy. But there is nothing about comedy (or about television) that prevents it from being an arena for moral pursuits on the part of the characters portrayed. In the case of *Seinfeld*, the cause of much of what is comic is that, just as in tragedy, the difficulties faced by the characters are often brought about by their own character flaws. And the characters must attempt to resolve their difficulties in the face of those very same flaws. This is just the way with life itself, and as in life, and unlike so many other television comedies, the characters in *Seinfeld* must make their way with no other moral compass than their own acquired moral judgments. Given the widespread belief, which I think is correct, that morally right action has some role in living a happy life, the desire for happiness, which the *Seinfeld* characters share, carries with it the concern with right action and living a moral life.

13
Virtue Ethics in TV's *Seinfeld*

AEON J. SKOBLE

Contemporary moral philosophy is in a troubled state. Kantians, utilitarians, and other theoretical camps continue to quarrel, while being beset by growing challenges from subjectivists and cultural relativists. To make matters worse, contemporary society seems to be in the thrall of an incoherent value system, wherein marijuana use often engenders longer jail time than murder, smokers are seen as more heinous than liars, and many people maintain, simultaneously, that they believe in God *and* that there is no such thing as right and wrong. What would it take to resolve the disputes within the academy and also enlighten a confused public? To do the former would require a splendid moral theory. To do the latter would require that powerful tool of mass learning, television. Not a documentary, not a high-band cable channel, but a popular program which reaches millions each week, one which can educate people even when they are intent on not learning anything. The moral theory which can best address our concerns is Aristotle's virtue ethics. The television program is NBC's popular comedy *Seinfeld*.

Aristotle's Virtue Ethics

Seinfeld has often been described as a comedy of manners, but it can actually be understood as an explication of Aristotelian moral theory. First, then, what is Aristotle's moral theory, and why is it a helpful one? Aristotle's *Nichomachean Ethics* is an example, indeed the *locus classicus,* of virtue ethics. In this moral paradigm, the important question is not so much "which acts are right and wrong?", but "what sort of character should I develop?"

Competing alternative theories are less satisfying in many respects. Utilitarianism, for example, is the view that the proper course is that which produces the greatest overall benefit for the greatest number of people—*act so as to produce the greatest good for the greatest number.* One common objection to this theory is that it seems to entail results which are so counterintuitive as to be unacceptable. For example, in its simplest form, the theory would allow us to inflict great suffering on a single innocent if it could benefit a larger number in a manner that outweighs that suffering. As a consequentialist theory, one which judges the moral acceptability of an action based on its consequences, utilitarianism holds that the end justifies the means, but our moral intuitions tell us that this is not always so. Utilitarianism is problematic, but, in any case, *Seinfeld*'s main characters can hardly be said to be exemplars of promoting the greatest good for the greatest number. The duty-based theory of Immanuel Kant, which exhorts us to follow the categorical imperative—*act so that you could will that the maxim of your action would become universal law*—is also problematic. Kant's theory implies that we have certain duties, but when we are faced with conflicting duties, it seems as though the only way to resolve them is to appeal to consequences. Because duty-based theories try to avoid the obvious problems with consequentialist theories, this is an unhappy turn. In any case, for a Kantian, right actions must proceed from a sense of duty, but while Jerry and his friends are often curious as to how to act, they seldom seem to be concerned with absolute moral duties.

Virtue ethics, in contrast to utilitarian and Kantian theories, is concerned with how to act, but focuses the inquiry on the character from which the actions proceed. This seems closer to the concerns of Jerry and George. The question "What is the right thing to do in this situation?" is often examined via a consideration of "what sort of person acts in such-and-such ways?" and "what would the wise person do in this situation?" These questions are the hallmarks of the Aristotelian approach, which is why the characters Jerry and George, in particular, can actually be understood as lessons in virtue ethics. While they sometimes seem to be concerned with "the rules," chiefly when they inquire into "protocol" or etiquette, closer investigation reveals that their primary concern is their character, what sort of person they should be. Of course, they are not perfect representatives of virtue ethics, but they nevertheless give us lessons in Greek wisdom.

For Aristotle, moral virtues are states of character one develops which, as they become more integral to one's being, help one to lead a happier, more fulfilled life. To acquire virtues, one needs to do three things: develop practical wisdom, discover and emulate positive role models, and practice acting well. Let us examine each of these in turn.

In Aristotle's theory, reason operates in more than one way. Reason tells me how to achieve a value or accomplish a goal efficiently, given any goal I might have. But reason can also tell me whether I should have the goals I have in the first place. For example, if I desire to eat cereal frequently, reason can tell me that I ought to have many bowls, much cereal, and ample milk in the house. But reason can also judge whether the desire for cereal is one which helps me live a better life overall, which, using skim milk, it does. Reason can judge the worthiness of a goal only with reference to a predominant goal. In other words, this-or-that value is good-for-me-to-have if and only if the pursuit of that value is conducive to my overall predominant value. On the Aristotelian view, there is such an overall predominant value, life, or more specifically, a flourishing or good life. One *naturally* desires to live a good life, and other desires must be shown to aid, not hinder, that larger goal.

Reason is also operative in deducing the proper course of action in a given situation. Aristotle recommends striving for the mean between extremes. Courage, for example, is said to be not only different from cowardice, but also from a rash faux-bravery. In other words, while cowardice is a vice, so is total fearlessness. The person who claims to be unafraid of *anything* is surely mistaken about the way the world works. One has ample reason to fear, say, angry grizzly bears, cannibalistic serial killers, or Crazy Joe Davola. Also, one must temper one's bravery with a consideration of circumstance—taking a foolish risk may look brave, but if it makes the situation worse, it's hardly virtuous. Now, this is no armchair philosophy. Aristotle says that one must learn how to be virtuous by practicing: by living through situations, and learning from experience.

Reason also leads us to the emulation of proper role models. The *phronemos*, or man of practical wisdom, is someone to be observed and learned from. The *phronemos* is not the same thing as a teacher, for one cannot teach virtues the way one teaches the alphabet. No one, for example, could "teach" Kramer to play golf, not even the caddy. To learn the game of golf, he had to study the fundamentals (such as angles, and body mechanics), observe good golfers, and practice, practice, practice. To learn virtue, one must study the fundamentals (such as the need for moderation between extremes), observe those who live well, and practice, practice, practice.

Jerry, George, and Aristotle?

Jerry and George frequently attempt to use reason to realize a goal, though sometimes not a terribly lofty goal. What is the best way to switch from dating one roommate to the other? When can I ask out someone who has just ended a relationship? How can I do as little work as possible without getting fired? But more to the point, they are often also concerned with how these short-term goals contribute to their overall well-being. For instance, when Jerry has an opportunity to have sex with multiple partners, he reflects not on the momentary pleasure such an experience would bring, but rather on what sort of person he would thus become: "I don't want to be an 'orgy guy,'" he realizes. Note the emphasis is not on rule-following, as in rule based ethics. A Kantian, for example, would ask whether he could rationally will it to be universal law that everyone have multiple sex partners. The emphasis is not on consequences either. A utilitarian, for example, would ask whether the greater number of people would be made happy by this act (which, in this case, they would). Jerry's emphasis, however, is not on the act itself at all; rather, the focus of his self-examination is what sort of person he would be were he to engage in this practice. What sort of character produces this action? Jerry does not want to be that kind of person, an "orgy guy." That lifestyle, with its bathrobes and cigarette holders, is not a lifestyle that Jerry sees as conducive to his long-term happiness.

In the episode entitled "The Lip Reader," Jerry decides to simply approach and ask out a beautiful woman, rather than engage in any subterfuge. George cautions against this, on the grounds that Jerry would therefore become a different sort of person, one of "*those* guys," as George articulately describes it. Note that George is not concerned here with the objective rightness or wrongness of the act, nor with the outcome of the act, but rather with what sort of person Jerry would thus become. Of course, George is extrapolating from his own fear of not being one of "those guys" that Jerry should not try to "cross over," but Jerry, judging that state to be one which would be conducive to his long-term well-being, chooses to ignore George's objection, correctly perceiving that the objection is not rational.

In addition to using reason to determine how to act, Aristotle says we ought to consider how a person of practical wisdom (a *phronemos*) would act in similar circumstances. The *phronemos* is supposed to be the role model for correct behavior. Here we can see another way virtue ethics manifests its influence in *Seinfeld*. For Jerry, of course, the primary role model is Superman. On occasion, Jerry seeks George's advice, typically on matters George might know better than Superman would, such as how to dump a girlfriend. But many times Jerry simply looks to and considers Superman. (The character Superman was, ironically, created by a person named Jerry, and the character Jerry was created by the real Jerry, perhaps suggesting that we are meant to see this connection.)

For George, who realizes he is "king of the idiots," the *phronemos* must be he who does the exact opposite of what George's instinct is to do. George comes to this realization in an episode entitled "The Opposite," and he is exactly right.[1] George may refer to himself as king of the idiots, but paradoxically, his recognition of his idiocy is what enables him to create his own *phronemos* by doing the opposite. This, of course, is a good update of the parable of Socrates and the Oracle. Socrates, who claimed to know nothing, was said by the Oracle at Delphi to

---

[1] For a different take on the viability of George's approach see Jason Holt, "The Costanza Maneuver: Is it Rational for George to do the Opposite?" in this volume.

be, in fact, the wisest man in Greece. After much searching and pestering of politicians, playwrights, and craftsmen, Socrates surmised that this could only mean that only those who *recognize* their own ignorance are in a position to acquire wisdom and hence virtue. This is precisely analogous to George's deduction in "The Opposite." If everything his instinct tells him is wrong, the opposite must be right. Jerry aids in the deductive process here, applying the logical axiom known as the Law of Excluded Middle. George had suggested the connection, but was unsure as to its logical validity. Jerry steps in and assures him that it is indeed correct, thus assuming the role of Oracle, or perhaps Socrates.[2] This is appropriate, for on many occasions, Jerry is actually George's role model, his *phronemos*. But Jerry cannot be a complete role model, as he is often confused himself. But the opposite-of-George would be a perfect source of guidance, given that George has had everything wrong to that point.

We see the proof of George's strategy immediately. He approaches a beautiful woman, and wins her affection. He refuses to be intimidated by obnoxious thugs in a theater, and instead intimidates them. He gets an interview with the New York Yankees, and when introduced to the owner of the team, George Steinbrenner, he proceeds to upbraid "the Boss" rather than kowtow to him. Steinbrenner rewards this bold candor by offering him a job. Of course, George does not continue this strategy, and frequently lapses into error as a result, confirming the theory.

Elaine, Kramer, and Newman: Not Wise

Elaine sometimes adopts a character-oriented approach, but she is less committed to it than George and Jerry, and frequently winds up in a jam as a result. For example, in "The Sponge," she tries to consider the character of her potential sex partners, surely a wise move (although she is actually motivated less by selectivity in her choice of men than by conservation of contraceptives). Other times, in fact more frequently, she does not consider the wise course, trying, for instance, to assassinate a

---

[2] See William Irwin, "Jerry and Socrates: The Examined Life?" in this volume.

noisy dog. She is often concerned with rules or "etiquette," suggesting that she may be thought of as a foil, an example of *not* using the Aristotelian approach. The trouble she gets into is often the result of sticking with rule-based approaches, which, as we have seen, often fail to account for the nuances which distinguish one situation from another. Elaine suffers accordingly. When she is guided by rules, she winds up dating the wrong man or stuck buying presents for people she doesn't like. When she tries to follow utilitarian strategies, this also backfires. She deduces that stopping to purchase Jujyfruits will only delay her trip to the hospital by a couple of minutes. But since this infuriates her injured boyfriend, he dumps her.

Kramer does not seem to participate in virtue ethics either. He lives so far outside the rest of the culture that, despite his friendship with Jerry and the others, he cannot take advantage of the social dialectic which helps produce virtue. He is more a figure of the Sartrean self-made self.[3] On Aristotle's account, the virtuous soul requires interaction with other virtuous souls for its development. The price Kramer pays is that he ends up friends with Newman, and even FDR (Franklin Delano Romanowski), who tries to kill him.

Although Newman clearly is not a *phronemos,* he is sometimes ironically invoked as one. When Elaine and Kramer have a dispute over ownership of a bicycle, they both defer to Newman's judgment. When there is some dispute as to whether Elaine's nipple is visible on a Christmas card photograph, they call in Newman to confirm. These appeals are clearly ironical because it is only Elaine and Kramer who appeal to Newman's alleged wisdom. George admits when pressed that Newman is "merry," but has no real use for him. Jerry regards Newman only as his nemesis. Since we can interpret both Jerry and George as participating in a Socratic investigation in search of Aristotelian virtue, Newman's role as nemesis serves to demonstrate one difficulty of virtue ethics. The *phronemos* must be chosen wisely, which is paradoxical in the sense that if we were wise enough to choose the right role-model, perhaps we would be wise enough not to need one. George is generally unimpressed by Newman; Jerry is wise enough to hold Newman in contempt;

---

[3] See Jennifer McMahon, "*Seinfeld,* Sartre, and Subjectivity," in this volume.

Kramer and Elaine actually defer to his judgment, indicating perhaps that they are less wise than Jerry and even George.

It is clear that Aristotelian virtue ethics presents a coherent moral theory, and a satisfactory alternative to utilitarian and Kantian theories. It stresses the use of both reason and experience in the development of character, producing the actions which lead one to flourish. What is less clear is whether Jerry and George can be seen as having learned as much as they might from their participation in this Socratic partnership in the search for virtue. That is, are they friends in the Aristotelian sense, augmenting and improving the virtues in one another? If the show were to have realized its full potential for moral education on the Aristotelian model, we ought to have seen a finale in which the characters translated their social dialectic into the good and happy life, rather than ending up in prison. But, perhaps this is a further subtlety. Recall that Socrates also ended up in prison (and was actually executed), and that Plato and Aristotle argued that happiness is a state of the soul, regardless of the political conditions in which one finds oneself. In the last hours of his life, Socrates persisted in philosophizing. When we last see the group in prison, Jerry is his usual self, doing his observational comedy routine. Perhaps we've made something out of nothing here, or perhaps there is a useful parallel to Greek wisdom, but one which was too subtle for the television audience.[4]

---

[4] See Eric Bronson, "Making Something out of Nothing: *Seinfeld*, Sophistry, and the Tao," in this volume.

14

The Final Episode: Is Doing Nothing Something?

THEODORE SCHICK, JR.

Two rules guided the writing of *Seinfeld*: no hugging and no learning. The final episode remained true to the first rule, but violated the second. Jerry and George were about to hug when they learned that their show *Jerry* (a show about nothing) was going to be produced by NBC. But they executed a mid-hug break off *(huggus interuptus?)* before the hug was consummated. The second rule went down in flames when we learned that Jerry's, George's, Elaine's, and Kramer's "selfishness, self-absorption, immaturity, and greed" was not only immoral, but also illegal in some jurisdictions.

In the series finale, NBC had granted Jerry the use of a company jet as compensation for keeping the pilot of his show on the shelf for five years. Jerry and Co. were on their way to Paris when Kramer started hopping around the plane trying to get some water out of his ears. His hopping landed him in the cockpit, and the plane went into a nosedive. Instead of crashing, however, it landed in the fictional town of Latham, Massachusetts where they witnessed a fat man being carjacked at gunpoint.[1] Kramer videotaped the event while George and

---

[1] One of the many rumors which circulated after the airing of the final episode was that we were supposed to interpret everything after the crash as the experience of the characters after death, "their final judgment." One of the ways

Elaine cracked jokes. "You see, the great thing about robbing a fat guy is the easy getaway. They can't really chase ya," mused Elaine. "He's actually doing him a favor. There's less money for him to buy food," quipped George. Jerry, who was holding a cell phone in his hand, could only manage, "Ah, that's a shame."

After the carjacker drove away, they were confronted by a police officer who charged them with breaking Latham's new "good Samaritan law"[2] which "requires you to help or assist anyone in danger as long as it is reasonable to do so." George was incredulous. "Why would we want to help someone?" he queried. "That's what nuns and Red Cross workers are for." The "New York Four," as they came to be known, were jailed, and Jerry was forced to eat cereal with only half his usual serving of milk. "This is the hardest thing I've ever had to do," he confessed.

The group asked Jackie Chiles, *Seinfeld*'s answer to Johnnie Cochran, to defend them. He took the case immediately. The good Samaritan law made no sense to him. "You don't have to help anybody," he declared. "That's what this country is all about." Although Chiles found the law "deplorable, unfathomable, and improbable," the jury didn't. After listening to a parade of character witnesses consisting of some of the most memorable minor characters from the show's past nine seasons, they found Jerry and Co. guilty of violating Latham's good Samaritan law. Judge Art Vandelay concurred with the verdict, claiming that their "callous indifference and utter disregard for everything that is good and decent rocked the foundation on which this society is built."

A grandiose claim? Undoubtedly. A totally unjustified claim? Perhaps not. To determine whether Jerry and Co. deserve to

---

Jerry Seinfeld and company had thought about ending the series is with all the characters being killed, perhaps driving off a bridge. In the end Jerry and the writers did not go with this approach, but this alternative interpretation allows us to play out some of what that would have involved. There is also a curious similarity between the closing shot, with the New York Four in prison, and Sartre's play *No Exit*. Is Hell other people, as Sartre's play suggests? Perhaps not for *Seinfeld*. For some interesting discussion of this connection see Jennifer McMahon, "*Seinfeld*, Sartre, and Subjectivity," in this volume.

[2] Note that there was an earlier *Seinfeld* episode entitled, "The Good Samaritan," in which Jerry tries to do the right thing but then ends up hitting on an attractive driver.

spend the next year behind bars, we'll have to explore the nature of our obligation to others. Are we our brother's keeper, and if so, how much of the rent do we have to pay?

Good Samaritans and Common Law

The Latham city good Samaritan law was supposedly modeled on the French law which reads:

> Anyone who, by their own actions, if there is no risk to themselves or another, can prevent a crime or physical harm and refuses to help shall be punished by five years imprisonment and a 500,000 franc fine.

> Anyone who refuses to come to the aid of a person in danger, if there is no risk to themselves or another, shall be punished by five years imprisonment and a 500,000-franc fine.[3]

This law dates back to 1941 and was recently invoked to bring charges against photographers at the scene of Princess Diana's death who allegedly took pictures of the crash instead of offering aid. A number of European countries have had such laws: Portugal (1867), the Netherlands (1881), Italy (1889 and 1930), Norway (1902), Russia (1903–17), Turkey (1926), Denmark (1930), Poland (1932), Germany (1935 and 1953), Romania (1938), Hungary (1948 and 1961), Czechoslovakia (1950), Belgium (1961), Switzerland (various dates), and Finland (1969).[4] Such statutes are not unheard of in the United States, however. Minnesota, Wisconsin, and Vermont have them. But the penalty for breaking these laws is much less severe than it is in France.

Good Samaritan laws are rare in the United States because our legal system is based on English Common Law, which takes the protection of individual liberty and self-interest to be paramount. Most laws in this tradition are designed to dissuade people from harming others or forcing them to do something against their will. Since bystanders do not injure anyone or take

---

[3] French Criminal Code, Article 223–26.
[4] Joel Feinberg, *Harm to Others: The Moral Limits of the Criminal Law* (Oxford: Oxford University Press, 1984), p. 256.

away their freedom, traditionally they have not been considered liable for failing to help. As Jackie Chiles informed the jury, "You cannot be a bystander and be guilty. Bystanders are by definition innocent. That is the nature of bystanding."

Laws protect our liberty and self-interest by granting us rights and imposing duties on others. Every right has a correlative duty. The rights granted to us by the United States Constitution are often referred to as "negative rights" because they impose on others a duty *not* to interfere with us in various ways. The right to life, for example, is often taken to be a negative right because it imposes on others a duty not to interfere with our lives. Everyone is free to do with their lives what they want as long as they don't interfere with anyone else's life. Your right to swing your arm extends only as far as my nose.

Some believe that the sole purpose of government is to protect our negative rights. Known as libertarians, they claim that government has only three legitimate functions: to provide a system of national defense, to provide a police system, and to provide a court system.[5] The armed services are needed to protect us from alien aggressors. The police force and court system are needed to protect us from each another. Spending tax dollars on any other programs, say the Libertarians, violates our right to do what we want with what we own. Libertarians would eliminate all government sponsored aid programs, like welfare and foreign aid, on the grounds that government has no business telling us how we should spend our money.

Libertarians would also eliminate all "no-victim" crimes because they are a contradiction in terms. Gambling, prostitution, and private drug use are considered no-victim crimes because those who engage in these activities do so of their own free will. According to Libertarianism, however, any activity that does not violate anyone's rights should not be outlawed. By legalizing no-victim crimes, libertarians believe that we would drastically reduce the crime rate. Police forces would no longer have to spend valuable time and money trying to enforce a mis-

---

[5] Some libertarians actually oppose even these three functions, thus becoming anarchists. See Aeon J. Skoble, "The Anarchism Controversy," in Tibor R. Machan and David B. Rasmussen eds., *Liberty for the Twenty-First Century: Contemporary Libertarian Thought* (Lanham, MD: Rowman and Littlefield, 1995), 77–96.

guided morality, and thus they could devote themselves to dealing with real crimes, such as murder, rape, theft, robbery, burglary, battery, fraud, and so on.

Those who espouse good Samaritan laws believe that our obligation to our fellow human beings goes beyond simply staying out of their hair. They believe that we have a duty to render assistance in certain circumstances. This view has some influential backers—most notably, Jesus. Jesus claimed that one way to achieve eternal life was to love thy neighbor as thyself. When asked, "Who is my neighbor?" he responded with the parable of the good Samaritan.

> A certain man went down from Jerusalem to Jericho, and fell among thieves, which stripped him of his raiment, and wounded him, and departed, leaving him half dead.
>
> And by chance there came down a certain priest that way: and when he saw him, he passed by on the other side.
>
> And likewise a Levite, when he was at the place, came and looked on him, and passed by on the other side.
>
> But a certain Samaritan, as he journeyed, came where he was; and when he saw him he had compassion on him.
>
> And went to him, and bound up his wounds, pouring in oil and wine, and set him on his own beast, and brought him to an inn, and took care of him.
>
> And on the morrow, when he departed, he took out two pence, and gave them to the host, and said unto him, "Take care of him; and whatsoever thou spendest more, when I come again, I will repay thee." (Luke 10:30–35)

After telling this story, Jesus said, "Go, and do thou likewise." It's unclear whether he considered being a good Samaritan a moral ideal that we should strive for, or a moral obligation that we should meet. Nevertheless, the parable does seem to suggest that others are owed more than just being left alone.

If we have a duty to help others in times of need, then in addition to negative rights, we also possess positive rights. A positive right imposes on others a duty to provide us with something. Interpreted positively, for example, the right to life imposes on others a duty to provide us with what we need to live.

This view that we are obligated to help others has spawned the political movement known as "communitarianism."

According to the communitarian platform:

> The exclusive pursuit of one's self-interest is not even a good pre-
> scription for conduct in the marketplace; for no social, political,
> economic, or moral order can survive that way. Some measure of
> caring, sharing, and being our brother's and sister's keeper is essen-
> tial if we are not all to fall back on an ever more expansive gov-
> ernment, bureaucratized welfare agencies, and swollen regulations,
> police, courts, and jails.[6]

Communitarians claim that we have an obligation to care for the
members of our community, especially when they cannot care
for themselves.

But what is the extent of this obligation? Everyone agrees that
it's a good thing to help people in need. But how much aid are
we obligated to give? The good Samaritan didn't just summon
the proper authorities. He bandaged, transported, and cared for
the traveler. He went way out of his way to be of assistance. Are
we morally obligated to make the same kind of sacrifices for
strangers in need?

Judith Jarvis Thomson thinks not. To prove her point, she
provides the following case:

> If I am sick unto death, and the only thing that will save my life is
> the touch of Henry Fonda's cool hand on my fevered brow, then
> all the same, I have no right to be given the touch of Henry Fonda's
> cool hand on my fevered brow.[7]

Thomson admits that it would be "frightfully nice" of Henry
Fonda to fly in and come to her aid (it would also be miracu-
lous since Henry Fonda is dead), but nevertheless, she believes
that Henry Fonda is under no obligation to do so. To require
Fonda to come to her bedside would violate his negative right
to do with his life what he wants to do. For Thomson, good
Samaritanism is a moral ideal, not a moral requirement.

---

[6] Amitai Etzioni, "The Responsive Communitarian Platform: Rights and
Responsibilities," *The Spirit of Community: The Reinvention of American
Society* (New York: Touchstone, 1993), pp. 259–260.
[7] Judith Jarvis Thomson, "A Defense of Abortion," in William Parent ed., *Rights,
Restitution, and Risk* (Cambridge: Harvard University Press, 1986), p. 8.

Minimally Decent Samaritans and Uncommon Law

There's an important distinction to be made between acts we are obligated to perform and acts that go above and beyond the call of duty. Non-obligatory but good acts are known as "supererogatory acts." Helping an old lady across the street, for example, is a supererogatory act. You are not obligated to help the old lady, but it sure would be nice.

Thomson claims that the good Samaritan's actions were supererogatory. He went above and beyond the call of duty in providing the traveler with medical care and lodging. In her view, then, we are not morally obligated to be good Samaritans.

But we are morally obligated to be "minimally decent Samaritans." To illustrate this concept, Thomson offers the following variation on the original Henry Fonda case:

> Suppose he [Henry Fonda] has only to walk across the room, place a hand briefly on my brow—and lo, my life is saved. Then surely he ought to do it, it would be indecent to refuse.[8]

Although Thomson allows that, in this case, Fonda ought to put his cool hand on her fevered brow, she doesn't want to go so far as to say that Fonda would be violating her rights if he didn't. For she considers it a "shocking idea that anyone's rights should fade away and disappear as it gets harder and harder to accord to them."[9] So even in this case, Thomson seems to consider Fonda's action supererogatory. But is it?

Supererogatory actions have traditionally been understood in two different ways. On the one hand, they have been considered to be harder to perform than ordinary duties. On the other, they have been considered to be acts "whose performance we praise but whose non-performance we do not condemn."[10] Fonda's walking across the room and touching Thomson's forehead, however, is not supererogatory in either of these two senses. It is not hard for him to do, and we certainly would condemn him if he didn't do it. So contrary to

---

[8] Ibid., p. 14.
[9] Ibid.
[10] Feinberg, p. 150.

what Thomson would have us believe, it looks as if Fonda does have a duty to help in the second case. He is under no obligation to be a good Samaritan—he doesn't have to fly in from the west coast to save her—but he is obligated to be a minimally decent Samaritan.

Consider a less fanciful example. Suppose you are walking down a lonely street and a child comes running up beside you, falls face down in a puddle, and doesn't move. Do you have a duty to reach down and, at least, turn the child's head? It would seem so. Such an action would not be difficult, and we would consider you a moral monster if you didn't do it. It would be no defense to claim that the child's falling is none of your business. Intuitively, then, the right to an easy rescue—a rescue that does not put the rescuer in any danger—is one that we seem to have.

Should we be legally obligated to be minimally decent Samaritans? Some have argued "No" on the grounds that we can't legislate morality. But we do so all the time. We pass laws against murder, rape, theft, assault, kidnapping, and so on, because these activities are immoral; they cause unnecessary suffering. One of the primary purposes of American law is to help prevent unnecessary suffering or harm to others. A good Samaritan law of the sort outlined above—a right to an easy rescue—would serve that purpose quite well. It is unnecessary for someone to suffer when another can prevent the suffering at no cost to themselves. So such a law may not be as un-American as Jackie Chiles would have us believe.

Even Libertarians should favor such a law. In their view, the purpose of the law is to promote our liberty and self-interest.[11] A right to an easy rescue would serve both of these purposes. It is in our self-interest to get an easy rescue when we need one. And knowing that we could expect one when needed would give us more freedom in planning our activities. So instead of limiting our liberty, good Samaritan laws may actually promote it.

---

[11] This is not to suggest that libertarians would necessarily be in favor of acting for the sake of another in this scenario, or would necessarily be against acting as a true Good Samaritan. The libertarian view is simply that there should be no law compelling people to act as Good Samaritans. Whether, in the absence of any such law, individuals decided to so act would just be up to them.

Against such a law, it could be argued that we should only be held responsible for what we cause, and since we did not cause whatever harm comes to those we fail to rescue, we shouldn't be held liable for not rescuing them. The principle that we can only be held responsible for what we cause does not hold universally, however. Transportation carriers, for example, can be held liable for harm that befalls their passengers even though they are not the cause of it. So the law does not maintain that we are legally responsible only for what we cause.

Nor are we morally responsible only for what we cause. James Rachels brings this out in the following two cases.

> In the first, Smith stands to gain a large inheritance if anything should happen to his six-year-old cousin. Smith sneaks into the bathroom and drowns the child, and then arranges things so that it will look like an accident.
>
> In the second, Jones also stands to gain if anything should happen to his six-year-old cousin. Like Smith, Jones sneaks in planning to drown the child in his bath. However, just as he enters the bathroom, Jones sees the child slip and hit his head, and fall face down in the water. Jones is delighted; he stands by, ready to push the child's head back under if it is necessary, but it is not necessary. With only a little thrashing about, the child drowns all by himself, "accidentally," as Jones watches and does nothing.[12]

Jones did not cause the death of his nephew; he was, so to speak, an innocent bystander. Smith, on the other hand, is a cold-blooded killer. If there were a significant moral difference between acting and failing to act, then what Jones did should be less morally reprehensible than what Smith did. But it isn't. Doing nothing can be something.

Jerry and Co. did wrong by not notifying the authorities. They had no obligation to try to stop the carjacking (for that could have put them in serious danger) but they could at least have picked up Jerry's cell-phone and dialed 911. Because they didn't, they fell below the standard of a minimally decent Samaritan, and for that they should be punished.

---

[12] James Rachels, "Active and Passive Euthanasia," *The New England Journal of Medicine 292* (9 January 1975), p. 79.

Crime and Character

Jerry and Co. broke the law—a law that deserves to be on the books. But are they bad people? The prosecutor thought so. "The big issue is character," he proclaimed. And to prove it, he paraded a seemingly endless stream of character witnesses in front of the jury. But as any good lawyer will tell you, evidence of character is generally inadmissible in a court of law. Unless it's relevant to proving an element of the crime, it should not be brought up. Jackie Chiles was right to object to the first character witness. But he should have objected to all of the rest of them as well.

Even if character evidence were relevant, however, Jackie Chiles could have done more than he did to rebut the testimony given. A lot of the incidents recounted seemed much worse than they actually were. Many were cases of mistaken perception. George is not a communist, contrary to what Steinbrenner testified. Elaine is not a slut despite the fact that she bought a case of contraceptive sponges. And Kramer is not a pimp, even though he was dressed like one when he was found with a prostitute. What's more, as any nun will tell you, there's nothing wrong with trying to be the master of your domain.

Of the four, Jerry committed the most serious crimes: stealing a loaf of bread, urinating in the parking garage, participating in a cockfight, and so forth. But is he a bad person? He certainly is not an evil person. He does not intentionally try to harm others. Nor is he a callous and indifferent person. He cares deeply for his friends and would do anything for them. In fact, his attempts to help them out are what often got him into trouble. His problem is not that he doesn't care, but that he cares too much.

Neither Jerry nor his friends are good Samaritans. They are not paragons of virtue. But neither are they paramours of vice. Their faults pale in comparison to those who are truly evil. Let them serve their time, but let us be clear about why they're serving it—not because they are bad people but because, in this one instance, they failed to do their duty.

What's the Deal with Episode Lists?

There are different ways of counting the number of episodes. I have chosen to count one-hour episodes, split into two episodes for syndication, as one. These episodes are indicated with an asterisk. The "Highlights of a Hundred" show (February 2, 1995) and the "Clip Show" have been omitted from the count.

Titles	Air Dates
1. "Good News, Bad News" (*The Seinfeld Chronicles*)	July 5, 1989
2. "The Stakeout"	May 31, 1990
3. "The Robbery"	June 7, 1990
4. "Male Unbonding"	June 14, 1990
5. "The Stock Tip"	June 21, 1990
6. "The Ex-Girlfriend"	January 23, 1991
7. "The Pony Remark"	January 30, 1991
8. "The Jacket"	February 6, 1991
9. "The Phone Message"	February 13, 1991
10. "The Apartment"	April 4, 1991
11. "The Statue"	April 11, 1991
12. "The Revenge"	April 18, 1991
13. "The Heart Attack"	April 25, 1991
14. "The Deal"	May 2, 1991
15. "The Baby Shower"	May 16, 1991
16. "The Chinese Restaurant"	May 23, 1991
17. "The Busboy"	June 26, 1991
18. "The Note"	September 18, 1991
19. "The Truth"	September 25, 1991

20.	"The Pen"	October 2, 1991
21.	"The Dog"	October 9, 1991
22.	"The Library"	October 16, 1991
23.	"The Parking Garage"	October 30, 1991
24.	"The Café"	November 6, 1991
25.	"The Tape"	November 13, 1991
26.	"The Nose Job"	November 20, 1991
27.	"The Stranded"	November 27, 1991
28.	"The Alternate Side"	December 4, 1991
29.	"The Red Dot"	December 11, 1991
30.	"The Subway"	January 8, 1992
31.	"The Pez Dispenser"	January 15, 1992
32.	"The Suicide"	January 29, 1992
33.	"The Fix-Up"	February 5, 1992
34.	"The Boyfriend"*	February 12, 1992
35.	"The Limo"	February 26, 1992
36.	"The Good Samaritan"	March 4, 1992
37.	"The Letter"	March 25, 1992
38.	"The Parking Space"	April 22, 1992
39.	"The Keys"	May 6, 1992
40.	"The Trip" Part I	August 12, 1992
41.	"The Trip" Part II	August 19, 1992
42.	"The Pitch/The Ticket"*	September 16, 1992
43.	"The Wallet"	September 23, 1992
44.	"The Watch"	September 30, 1992
45.	"The Bubble Boy"	October 7, 1992
46.	"The Cheever Letters"	October 28, 1992
47.	"The Opera"	November 4, 1992
48.	"The Virgin"	November 11, 1992
49.	"The Contest"	November 18, 1992
50.	"The Airport"	November 25, 1992
51.	"The Pick"	December 16, 1992
52.	"The Movie"	January 6, 1993
53.	"The Visa"	January 27, 1993
54.	"The Shoes"	February 4, 1993
55.	"The Outing"	February 11, 1993
56.	"The Old Man"	February 18, 1993
57.	"The Implant"	February 25, 1993
58.	"The Junior Mint"	March 18, 1993
59.	"The Smelly Car"	April 15, 1993
60.	"The Handicap Spot"	May 13, 1993

61.	"The Pilot"*	May 20, 1993
62.	"The Mango"	September 16, 1993
63.	"The Puffy Shirt"	September 23, 1993
64.	"The Glasses"	September 30, 1993
65.	"The Sniffing Accountant"	October 7, 1993
66.	"The Bris"	October 14, 1993
67.	"The Lip Reader"	October 28, 1993
68.	"The Non-Fat Yogurt"	November 4, 1993
69.	"The Barber"	November 11, 1993
70.	"The Masseuse"	November 18, 1993
71.	"The Cigar Store Indian"	December 9, 1993
72.	"The Conversion"	December 16, 1993
73.	"The Stall"	January 6, 1994
74.	"The Dinner Party"	February 3, 1994
75.	"The Marine Biologist"	February 10, 1994
76.	"The Pie"	February 17, 1994
77.	"The Stand-In"	February 24, 1994
78.	"The Wife"	March 17, 1994
79.	"The Raincoats"*	April 28, 1994
80.	"The Fire"	May 5, 1994
81.	"The Hamptons"	May 12, 1994
82.	"The Opposite"	May 19, 1994
83.	"The Chaperone"	September 22, 1994
84.	"The Big Salad"	September 29, 1994
85.	"The Pledge Drive"	October 6, 1994
86.	"The Chinese Woman"	October 13, 1994
87.	"The Couch"	October 27, 1994
88.	"The Gymnast"	November 3, 1994
89.	"The Soup"	November 10, 1994
90.	"The Mom & Pop Store"	November 17, 1994
91.	"The Secretary"	December 8, 1994
92.	"The Race"	December 15, 1994
93.	"The Switch"	January 5, 1995
94.	"The Label Maker"	January 19, 1995
95.	"The Scofflaw"	January 26, 1995
96.	"The Beard"	February 9, 1995
97.	"The Kiss Hello"	February 16, 1995
98.	"The Doorman"	February 23, 1995
99.	"The Jimmy"	March 16, 1995
100.	"The Doodle"	April 6, 1995
101.	"The Fusilli Jerry"	April 27, 1995

102.	"The Diplomat's Club"	May 4, 1995
103.	"The Face Painter"	May 11, 1995
104.	"The Understudy"	May 18, 1995
105.	"The Engagement"	September 21, 1995
106.	"The Postponement"	September 28, 1995
107.	"The Maestro"	October 5, 1995
108.	"The Wink"	October 12, 1995
109.	"The Hot Tub"	October 19, 1995
110.	"The Soup Nazi"	November 2, 1995
111.	"The Secret Code"	November 9, 1995
112.	"The Pool Guy"	November 16, 1995
113.	"The Sponge"	December 7, 1995
114.	"The Gum"	December 14, 1995
115.	"The Rye"	January 4, 1996
116.	"The Caddy"	January 25, 1996
117.	"The Seven"	February 1, 1996
118.	"The Cadillac"*	February 8, 1996
119.	"The Shower Head"	February 15, 1996
120.	"The Doll"	February 22, 1996
121.	"The Friar's Club"	March 7, 1996
122.	"The Wig Master"	April 4, 1996
123.	"The Calzone"	April 25, 1996
124.	"The Bottle Deposit"*	May 2, 1996
125.	"The Wait Out"	May 9, 1996
126.	"The Invitations"	May 16, 1996
127.	"The Foundation"	September 19, 1996
128.	"The Soul Mate"	September 26, 1996
129.	"The Bizarro Jerry"	October 3, 1996
130.	"The Little Kicks"	October 10, 1996
131.	"The Package"	October 17, 1996
132.	"The Fatigues"	October 31, 1996
133.	"The Checks"	November 7, 1996
134.	"The Chicken Roaster"	November 14, 1996
135.	"The Abstinence"	November 21, 1996
136.	"The Andrea Doria"	December 19, 1996
137.	"The Little Jerry"	January 9, 1997
138.	"The Money"	January 16, 1997
139.	"The Comeback"	January 30, 1997
140.	"The Van Buren Boys"	February 6, 1997
141.	"The Susie"	February 13, 1997
142.	"The Pothole"	February 20, 1997

143.	"The English Patient"	March 13, 1997
144.	"The Nap"	April 10, 1997
145.	"The Yada Yada"	April 24, 1997
146.	"The Millennium"	May 1, 1997
147.	"The Muffin Tops"	May 8, 1997
148.	"The Summer of George"	May 15, 1997
149.	"The Butter Shave"	September 25, 1997
150.	"The Voice"	October 2, 1997
151.	"The Serenity Now"	October 9, 1997
152.	"The Blood"	October 16, 1997
153.	"The Junk Mail"	October 30, 1997
154.	"The Merv Griffen Show"	November 6, 1997
155.	"The Slicer"	November 13, 1997
156.	"The Betrayal"	November 20, 1997
157.	"The Apology"	December 11, 1997
158.	"The Strike"	December 18, 1997
159.	"The Dealership"	January 8, 1998
160.	"The Reverse Peephole"	January 15, 1998
161.	"The Cartoon"	January 29, 1998
162.	"The Strongbox"	February 5, 1998
163.	"The Wizard"	February 26, 1998
164.	"The Burning"	March 19, 1998
165.	"The Bookstore"	April 9, 1998
166.	"The Frogger"	April 23, 1998
167.	"The Maid"	April 30, 1998
168.	"The Puerto Rican Day"	May 7, 1998
169.	"The Finale" (With the Clip Show)	May 14, 1998

Who Are These Philosophers?

Thales (ca. 624–546 B.C.E.)

"All things are full of gods and have a share of soul."

Anaximander (ca. 611–546 B.C.E.)

"From what source things arise, to that they return of necessity when they are destroyed; for they suffer punishment and make reparation to one another for their injustice according to the order of time."

Lao Tzu (born ca. 604 B.C.E.)

"He who knows does not speak. He who speaks does not know. Close the mouth."

Anaximenes (ca.585–528 B.C.E.)

"Air is the principle of existing things; for from it all things come-to-be and into it they are again dissolved."

Buddha (560–480 B.C.E.)

"All humanity is sick. I come therefore to you as a physician who has diagnosed this universal disease and is prepared to cure it."

Confucius (ca. 551–479 B.C.E.)

"Great man is always at ease; petty man is always on edge."

Heraclitus (died ca. 510–480 B.C.E.)

"The real constitution of things is accustomed to hide itself."

Parmenides (515–445 B.C.E.)

"For never shall this be proved, that things that are not, are."

Socrates (470–399 B.C.E.)

"The unexamined life is not worth living."

Plato (428/7–348/7 B.C.E.)

"The feeling of wonder is the touchstone of the philosopher, and all philosophy has its origins in wonder."

Aristotle (384–322 B.C.E.)

"All men by nature desire to know."

Epicurus (341–270 B.C.E.)

"We recognize pleasure as the first and natural good; starting from pleasure we accept or reject; and we return to this as we judge every good thing, trusting this feeling of pleasure as our guide."

Epictetus (50–130)

"It is not the things themselves that disturb men, but their judgments about these things."

Marcus Aurelius (121–180)

"Everything that happens is as normal and as expected as the spring rose or the summer fruit; this is true of sickness, death, slander, intrigue, and all other things that delight or trouble foolish men."

Augustine (354–430)

"Even that which is called evil, when it is regulated and out in its own place, only enhances our admiration of the good."

Anselm (1033–1109)

"You exist so truly, Lord my God, that You cannot even be thought not to exist."

Thomas Aquinas (1225–1274)

"Therefore some intelligent being exists by whom all natural things are directed to their end; and this being we call God."

Francis Bacon (1561–1626)

"And not only must we look for and acquire a greater number of experiments, and ones of a different kind from those used hitherto, but also a quite different method, order, and procedure must be introduced for the continuation and furtherance of experience."

Thomas Hobbes (1588–1679)

"[In the state of nature] the life of man [is] solitary, poor, nasty, brutish, and short."

René Descartes (1596–1650)

"Anything which admits of the slightest doubt I will set aside just as if I had found it to be wholly false."

Baruch Spinoza (1632–1677)

"I do not know how to teach philosophy without becoming a disturber of the peace."

John Locke (1632–1704)

"The natural liberty of man is to be free from any superior power on earth, and not to be under the will or legislative authority of man, but only have the law of nature for his rule."

Gottfried Leibniz (1646–1716)

"The soul follows its own laws, and the body likewise follows its own laws; and they agree with each other in virtue of the pre-established harmony between all substances, since they are all representations of one and the same universe."

George Berkeley (1685–1753)

"To be is to be perceived."

David Hume (1711–1776)

"If we take in our hand any volume . . . let us ask, Does it contain any abstract reasoning conerning quantity or number? No. Does it contain any experimental reasoning concerning matter of fact and existence? No. Commit it then to the flames: for it can contain nothing but sophistry and illusion."

Immanuel Kant (1724–1804)

"But though all our knowledge begins with experience, it does not follow that it all arises from experience."

G.W.F. Hegel (1770–1831)

"What is rational is actual and what is actual is rational."

Arthur Schopenhauer (1788–1860)

"Every man takes the limits of his own field of vision for the limits of the world."

John Stuart Mill (1806–1873)

"It is better to be a human being dissatisfied than a pig satisfied; better to be Socrates dissatisfied than a fool satisfied."

Søren Kierkegaard (1813–1855)

"Had I to carve an inscription on my grave, I would ask for none other than 'that individual'."

Karl Marx (1818–1883)

"The philosophers have only interpreted the world, in various ways: the point is to change it."

Charles Sanders Peirce (1839–1914)

"Few persons care to study logic, because everybody conceives himself to be proficient enough in the art of reasoning already. But I observe that this satisfaction is limited to one's own ratiocination, and does not extend to that of other men."

William James (1842–1910)

"My first act of freedom will be to believe in free will."

Friedrich Nietzsche (1844–1900)

"What is good? All that enhances the feeling of power, the will to power, and the power itself in man."

Gottlob Frege (1848–1925)

"It is certainly praiseworthy to try to make clear to oneself as far as possible the sense one associates with a word. But here we must not forget that not everything can be defined."

Edmund Husserl (1859–1938)

"To the things themselves."

Henri Bergson (1859–1941)

"The eye sees only what the mind is prepared to comprehend."

John Dewey (1859–1952)

"The sense of an extensive and underlying whole is the context of every experience and it is the essence of sanity."

Alfred North Whitehead (1861–1947)

"Thus nature is a structure of evolving process. The reality is the process."

Bertrand Russell (1872–1970)

"Scepticism, while logically impeccable, is psychologically impossible, and there is an element of frivolous insincerity in any philosophy which pretends to accept it."

G.E. Moore (1873–1958)

"If I am asked 'What is good?' my answer is good is good, and that is the end of the matter."

Ludwig Wittgenstein (1889–1951)

"What is your aim in philosophy? —To show the fly the way out of the fly-bottle."

Martin Heidegger (1889–1976)

"Is being a mere word and its meaning a vapor, or does what is designated by the word 'being' hold within it the historical destiny of the West?"

Gilbert Ryle (1900–1976)

"Learning *how* or improving in ability is not like learning *that* or acquiring information."

Karl Popper (1902–1995)

"I propose to replace the question of the sources of our knowledge by the entirely different question: 'How can we hope to detect and eliminate error?'"

Jean-Paul Sartre (1905-1980)

"Thus existentialism's first move is to make every man aware of what he is and to make the full responsibility of his existence rest on him."

Simone de Beauvoir (1908–1986)

"A Woman is not born . . . she is created."

W.V.O. Quine (1908–)

"What the indeterminancy of translation shows is that the notion of propositions as sentence meanings is untenable. What the empirical underdetermination of global science shows is that there are various defensible ways of conceiving the world."

NOTES ON THE SCRIPT WRITERS, AKA THE CONTRIBUTORS TO THIS VOLUME
Who Are These People?

DANIEL BARWICK is Assistant Professor of Philosophy and Honors Program Co-ordinator at the State University of New York College of Technology at Alfred. His publications include works in the philosophy of mind, metaphysics, and bioethics. *Dan supplements his income by renting his villa in Tuscany.*

ERIC BRONSON is Adjunct Professor of Philosophy at Berkeley College of New York, and has produced a feature-length documentary film entitled *My Lazy White Friends. Eric is fond of boasting, "I practice what I preach and do Nothing."*

MARK T. CONARD is a fiction writer, philosopher, and Steppenwolf dwelling in Philadelphia. His publications on Kant and Nietzsche have appeared in *Philosophy Today* and the *Southern Journal of Philosophy*. His article "Symbolism, Meaning, and Nihilism in Quentin Tarantino's *Pulp Fiction*" was published in *Philosophy Now. Unfortunately, nothing personal can be said about Mark. It seems he sold his biography to J. Peterman, who would not grant permission to reprint any part of it.*

ROBERT A. EPPERSON teaches Philosophy at Auburn University. He works primarily in ethics, epistemology, and logic, *but when asked what he does often responds, "I'm an architect."*

JORGE J.E. GRACIA is Samuel P. Capen Chair and SUNY Distinguished Professor of Philosophy at the State University of New York at Buffalo. His publications include *Philosophy and*

Its History (1992), *A Theory of Textuality* (1995), and *Texts* (1996), among many others. His book *Hispanic/Latino Identity* is in press, and he is currently writing a book on the interpretation of divinely revealed texts. *Jorge is Kramer's favorite contributor to this volume because he is the genuine article, a real Cuban!*

JASON HOLT is Assistant Professor of Philosophy at the University of Manitoba. His publications include "A Comprehensivist Theory of Art" in the *British Journal of Aesthetics*, "Superassertibility and Asymptotic Truth" in *Dialogue*, and a book of poetry entitled *Feeling Fine in Kafka's Burrow* (AB Collector, 1994). *He has never been in a Woody Allen movie.*

WILLIAM IRWIN is Assistant Professor of Philosophy at King's College. He is the author of *Intentionalist Interpretation: A Philosophical Explanation and Defense.* He has also published articles and reviews on hermeneutics, Sartre, Plato, philosophy of law, and philosophical pedagogy. *He enjoys spending time with cousin Jeffrey, eating chocolate bobka, smoking Cuban cigars, cherishing the cabin, and mixing metaphors.*

KELLY DEAN JOLLEY is Associate Professor of Philosophy at Auburn University. He has published articles in *Philosophical Quarterly, Philosophical Investigations,* and *James Joyce Quarterly. Warning: Kelly's articles seem better or worse depending on the lighting.*

NORAH MARTIN is Assistant Professor of Philosophy at the University of Portland. She has recently co-edited (with Peter Ludlow) a collection of essays on externalism and self-knowledge, and has published in the *Journal of Medicine and Philosophy. Norah's current research focuses on the existence of a mutant race of pig men and the ethics of eating Junior Mints in the operating room.*

JENNIFER MCMAHON is Assistant Professor of Philosophy at Centre College. She has published on Sartre and aesthetics. *Both existentialist and equestrian, Jennifer spends most of her time thinking about "nothing," and experiencing the nausea that results from feeding her horses a steady diet of Beefarino.*

THEODORE SCHICK, JR. is Professor of Philosophy at Muhlenberg College. He is co-author (with Lewis Vaughn) of *How to Think about Weird Things: Critical Thinking for a New Age and Doing Philosophy: An Introduction through Thought Experiments. Ted insists on eating his M&M's with a spoon.*

AEON J. SKOBLE is Assistant Professor of Philosophy at West Point. He has published articles on political philosophy, moral philosophy, and the subversive influence of *Forrest Gump. Aeon enjoys reading Glamour magazine.*

SARAH E. WORTH is Assistant Professor of Philosophy at Furman University. She specializes in ancient philosophy and aesthetics, and has published in the *British Journal of Aesthetics. Sarah would like to echo Elaine in saying, "I'm not a lesbian. I hate men, but I'm not a lesbian . . . Not that there's anything wrong with that."*

Index of Everything